TACKLING BULLYING IN ATHLETICS

Best Practices for Modeling Appropriate Behavior

Meline Kevorkian and
Robin D'Antona

ROWMAN & LITTLEFIELD EDUCATION
A division of
ROWMAN & LITTLEFIELD PUBLISHERS, INC.
Lanham • New York • Toronto • Plymouth, UK

Published by Rowman & Littlefield Education
A division of Rowman & Littlefield Publishers, Inc.
A wholly owned subsidiary of The Rowman & Littlefield Publishing Group, Inc.
4501 Forbes Boulevard, Suite 200, Lanham, Maryland 20706
http://www.rowmaneducation.com

Estover Road, Plymouth PL6 7PY, United Kingdom

Copyright © 2010 by Meline Kevorkian and Robin D'Antona

All rights reserved. No part of this book may be reproduced in any form or by any electronic or mechanical means, including information storage and retrieval systems, without written permission from the publisher, except by a reviewer who may quote passages in a review.

British Library Cataloguing in Publication Information Available

Library of Congress Cataloging-in-Publication Data

Kevorkian, Meline M., 1968–
  Tackling bullying in athletics : best practices for modeling appropriate behavior / Meline Kevorkian and Robin D'Antona.
    p. cm.
  Includes bibliographical references and index.
  ISBN 978-1-60709-379-4 (cloth : alk. paper) — ISBN 978-1-60709-380-0 (pbk. : alk. paper) — ISBN 978-1-60709-381-7 (electronic)
  1. Sports—Psychological aspects. 2. Athletics—Psychological aspects. 3. Bullying. 4. Bullying—Prevention. 5. Aggressiveness. I. D'Antona, Robin, 1946– II. Title.
  GV706.4.K48 2010
  796.01—dc22   2010023013

∞™ The paper used in this publication meets the minimum requirements of American National Standard for Information Sciences—Permanence of Paper for Printed Library Materials, ANSI/NISO Z39.48-1992.

Printed in the United States of America

This book is dedicated to
Simon Francis D'Antona
1979–1993

CONTENTS

Foreword		vii
1	Why Care? 10 Win, 1 Loss Season	1
2	Why Bullying Prevention?	9
3	Athletes: The View from the Playing Field	23
4	Coaches: The View from the Locker Room	37
5	Fans: The View from the Grandstands	51
6	The Playbook: Best Practices—Prevention	63
7	The Playbook: Best Practices—Intervention	71
Final Thoughts on Preventing Bullying in Athletics		81
References		85
About the Authors		91

FOREWORD

If you are picking up this book, perhaps you are a coach, the parent of an athlete, a recreation director, a school administrator, or even the athlete about whom the authors are concerned. You may be saying to yourself, "Who needs another book on bullying?"

The authors are, without a doubt, experts in the field of bullying prevention. Yet more than that, they are deeply and personally determined to protect young people harmed, sometimes fatally, by the target-aggressor-bystander bullying dynamic. This book offers concrete information to help you understand how bullying plays out, in its more obvious and most insidious forms. Even more important, it provides concrete, research-based suggestions on how to reduce or even prevent bullying.

The authors have written a straightforward, highly readable book about bullying in athletics. They have purposely chosen not to delve into the annals of athletes and sexual harassment or the details of the law known as Title IX that plays a central role in supporting females in sports and in preventing sexual harassment. But if, after reading this book, you want to learn more, I urge you to dig further.

No book can give the secret ingredient that enables us—whether adults or young athletes—to intervene when bullying occurs and to take steps to prevent it in the first place. That secret ingredient is, quite simply, courage. What is courage? Why is it needed?

While athletics offer great tests of physical courage, stamina, determination, and discipline, there is another very different form of courage. Moral courage is the willingness to do what is right in the face of pressure from peers, parents, community leaders, supervisors, team members, and so on. Bullying and harassment (a form of bias-based bullying with roots in civil rights laws) thrive when adult authority figures fail to identify and intervene, choosing to ignore or justify such behaviors. Teachers, coaches, administrators, and parents are role models. When young people, athletes or not, see these adult authority figures (and this means you) displaying moral courage, they too learn to follow that path.

Several years ago, a serious bullying incident occurred during a summer training session for a fall high school sport. Out of a large group of bystanders, only one boy backed up the target's story. His father told him he had to do so, because it was the right thing to do. None of the other bystanders spoke up until he did. Their parents had urged them to remain silent. Legal charges were brought and the athletes who had committed the acts were removed from the school. The boy who spoke up was an "upstander," not a bystander.

The path of moral courage is not an easy one for adults or for young people. If it were, there would be far less bullying and probably far less violence. The culture that promotes the ideas "I don't want to get involved" and "I don't want to be a snitch" is not uncommon among young people. But when adults cry out against this culture, we need to look first at ourselves. Are we ignoring or justifying behaviors, such as bullying and harassment, because we lack the moral courage to follow the guidelines in *Tackling Bullying in Athletics*?

Randy Ross, MS, MA
The Education Alliance at Brown University
April 2010

1

WHY CARE?
10 WIN, 1 LOSS SEASON

HOW EXTENSIVE IS IT?
FROM SHAKING IT OFF TO SUICIDE

On Saturday, September 25, 1993, after Simon, a 14-year-old high school freshman, and his three friends attended a home varsity football game, they went to one of the boys' homes. There were many varied reports of what was going on and what they were actually doing that afternoon. They were full of fun and happy to be part of the football team—even if only as members of the freshman squad.

According to one account, they were feeling frisky and they went to the local supermarket, which was located in the center of town. They were parading up and down the supermarket aisle laughing and having fun in a way that adolescent boys think is funny. One of the boys wore a pair of underpants on his head. The boys were playful, acting silly, and laughing at this juvenile stunt. However, when they met a former teacher in the supermarket, they apparently felt embarrassed and claimed they were being hazed. The hazing component may or may not have been true.

Months later, investigations never confirmed nor refuted this statement. Regardless, that claim set up a chain of events that would lead to extreme bullying behavior that would end in tragedy. Once the report of what happened in that supermarket that Saturday afternoon became known to the members of the varsity football team, the boys were subjected to threats, bullying, exclusion, and other cruel behaviors that would become unbearable. Their dreams of participating in football were dashed. It was September of their freshman year and they had become outcasts in a world they had only just entered.

The chain of events began when the teacher reported the incident to the athletic director, who then arbitrarily decided that it was probably a prank the older football players had played on the younger boys. He instructed the head coach to look into the incident but to keep it quiet. The coaches consulted with other coaches, administrators, students, and parents—but not with the parents of the freshman boys involved.

By Tuesday, the football team and everyone connected with the team were buzzing about the alleged incident. The varsity players let Simon and his friends know they would handle the situation in their own way. When these freshman boys went to practice, the others, including upperclassmen and the assistant coaches, constantly yelled at and mistreated them. Even when Simon managed to run the ball through the line for a 10-yard gain, he was berated and made to feel that he could not do anything right.

The varsity football players continued to threaten the boys in the school hallways, the cafeteria, and at practice. In one instance in particular, one of the varsity players looked at Simon, put a hand to his own temple as if it was a gun and pulled the imaginary trigger. Then Simon reportedly told his friend, "They're going to get us. We're dead."

When Simon told his parents, it was already too late. He was frightened and feeling hopeless because he truly believed his high school athletic career was over. When he got home that afternoon, his father, a high school guidance counselor, was already there. After a brief conversation with his dad in which he was unable to convey the urgency and desperateness of his feelings, he went to his room to do his homework. Less than an hour later his father found him hanging in the family room. Simon died six weeks later, never having regained consciousness.

After this incident, the usual assumptions were made. People said that he must have been depressed, distant, troubled, or misunderstood. Was he impulsive, others asked. Because Simon D'Antona was my son, we know for a certainty that these theories were not true. In fact we later learned that this was a case of situational suicide brought on by bullying and harassment Simon received during that week in September of his freshman year in high school. It was clear that a terrible tragedy occurred between him and the boys that bullied him that week. It is so sad that bullying behaviors in the athletic setting are not only tolerated but also accepted.

Simon's death having no other apparent explanation, the culpability for this terrible tragedy was attributed to the victim and his family rather than the bullying. However, six years after Simon's death the infamous mass shooting incident on the campus of Columbine High School in Littleton, Colorado, started a national discussion about bullying. Today we know that suicide, which is the fourth leading cause of death for 14- to 17-year-olds, can be a direct result of bullying.

In fact, suicide that is a result of bullying now has its own name, bullycide. This word was coined by a group of parents who are survivors of suicide. The frequency and commonality of this occurrence brought them together to form a group that has grown into Bully Police, a well-recognized national organization whose mission is to wipe out bullying behavior. While suicide certainly is an extreme outcome of bullying behavior, there is much suffering that happens on a regular basis to the young people and even young athletes of today.

THE PROBLEM OF BULLYING

Research has suggested that many students are and will continue to be bullied in schools around the world (Burns, 2006; Dake, Price, & Telljohann, 2003; Eisenberg, Neumark-Sztainer, & Perry, 2003; GLSEN, 2001; Kuntsche et al., 2006; Lyznicki, McCaffree, & Robinowitz, 2004; Schnohr & Niclasen, 2006). According to Lipson (2001), in a national sample of students ages 8 to 11, 83 percent of girls and 79 percent of boys reported having experienced some sort of harassment in their schools.

Approximately 60 percent reported that both physical and nonphysical harassment occurred "under the teacher's nose." In a study conducted by Nickelodeon (2001), 74 percent of 7- to 11-year-olds and 86 percent of 12- to 15-year-olds indicated that children were bullied or teased in their schools. Dake, Price, and Telljohann (2003) found that victimized children tend to become more school avoidant after being bullied. Bullying is a school safety issue. Students who were bullied weekly were 60 percent more likely to carry a weapon to school, 70 percent more likely to be in frequent fights, and 30 percent more likely to be injured than students who were not bullied (Lyznicki et al., 2004).

DEFINITION OF BULLYING

Kevorkian (2006) defined bullying as a set of purposeful physical and emotional actions that have the potential to cause long-term damage, are carried out repeatedly, are intended to injure, and involve an imbalance of power. A general definition of bullying includes repeated exposure to negative actions by one or more students over time (Olweus, 1994). Olweus further defined a negative action as a purposeful attempt to injure or inflict discomfort on another, through either words, physical contact, gestures, or exclusion from a group. Beran and Shapiro (2005) referred to bullying as repetitive aggression directed at a peer who is unable to defend himself or herself.

While there is much discussion about bullying behavior and it has been the center of recent tragedies, there seems to be confusion about exactly what bullying behavior is. The word *bullying* seems to be overused and confused with other types of aggressive, harassing, and assaultive behavior. Three key factors that help separate out bullying from other types of inappropriate behaviors are that it is:

1. Intentional
2. Repeated
3. Power-based

BYSTANDERS

Research supports the concept that we must empower bystanders to assist their peers if we really want to reduce bullying in our schools (Lodge & Frydenberg, 2005). In regard to bystanders, Coloroso (2005) wrote that to break the bullying cycle, we must help change the role of the bystander. Entenman, Murnen, and Hendricks (2005) suggested that "a bystander may be afraid to get involved, not know what to do, or be coerced by the bully not to tell" (p. 355). Lodge and Frydenberg (2005) discussed that bullying behavior that has no consequences for the bully and little to no intervention may cause children to become nervous, fearful, and uncomfortable at school.

All children are exposed to bullying—either as a bully, victim, or bystander—and most of the time this goes unaddressed by adults (Hoard, 2007). Furthermore, we have learned that bystanders suffer when they witness bullying behavior. They feel frightened, guilty, and worried that they may be at risk of being victimized. Research has emphasized that teaching bystanders how to respond to bullying situations can be crucial in reducing bullying.

VICTIMS

Children may be victimized regarding their sexual identity (Williams et al., 2005). This can mean that they are bullied because of their sexual orientation. That bullying can be either real or perceptual. *Fag* and *gay* are common words as early as elementary school and these names and attacks on sexual identity can be very hurtful, particularly for adolescents who are struggling to understand their own emerging sexual identity.

Additionally, children are victimized by their social status, special needs, or being viewed as different (Kevorkian, 2006). Victims tend to be less accepted by peers and to be more insecure and withdrawn (Hodges et al., 1999). Victims of bullying behavior report a myriad of distress symptoms. Children who are bullied are at risk for a variety of mental health problems, the most common being depression (Salmon, James, & Smith, 1998).

Victimized children were more likely to exhibit sleep problems, bed-wetting, headaches, stomachaches, and feeling tense or nervous. Fekkes et al. (2006) indicated that victimization causes an increase in health problems such as headaches, abdominal pain, anxiety, and depression. This supports the hypothesis that the stress of victimization may cause the development of somatic and psychological health problems. "The effects of bullying are rarely obvious, and it is unlikely that a child will complain to the physician of bullying or being bullied" (Lyznicki et al., 2004).

BULLIES

Coloroso (2005) stated, "Bullies come in all shapes and sizes, big, small, bright, and not so bright. Some are popular and some are disliked."

Brinson (2005) found that girls also bully boys. Frisén, Jonsson, and Persson (2007) found that many perceptions exist for adolescents as to why kids bully, including that kids who bully have low self-esteem. Spade (2007) discussed that bullying tends to occur during unstructured and unsupervised periods of time. Girls who bully "use more verbal and psychological techniques such as verbal harassment, exclusion from activities, name-calling, and initiation of rumors" (Entenman et al., 2005).

SCHOOL CLIMATE AND BULLYING PREVENTION

"School climate can enhance or impair student development and achievement" (Wilson, 2004). Positive school climate (established by interest, concern, and support for all students) is correlated with student achievement (Halawah, 2005). Respect for all members of the school community and a positive relationship between students and teachers are common characteristics in schools where students report a positive school climate (Wilson, 2004). Hickey (2003) discussed participation in sports and other extracurricular activities as an aspect of school connectedness.

Many children do not let an adult know if they have been bullied. This decision to disclose is multidetermined; however, the teacher's response is likely to be a key factor in choosing to disclose victimization (Craig, Pepler, & Blais, 2007). Students report that teachers do not consistently intervene to stop bullying (Atlas & Pepler, 1998). Research supports that physical abuse is seen as more severe than verbal or emotional abuse and physical conflicts are seen as bullying even when they did not match the definition (Hazler & Miller, 2001). Dake and colleagues (2003) reported a need to increase knowledge and awareness regarding the problem of bullying.

Additionally, a whole-school approach to bullying prevention was indicated as necessary for successful bullying prevention efforts. School-wide interventions are supported to include working with bystanders, who make up the majority of a population, rather than working with bullies or victims only. Salmivalli, Kaukiainen, and Voeten (2005) and Chibbaro (2007) suggested including steps that bystanders can take to report and respond to cyberbullying. Coloroso (2005) stated, "Bullying is effectively challenged when the majority stands up against cruel acts of the minority. Since much of the bullying occurs 'beneath the radar' of adult supervision, kids can be a potent force against bullies" (p. 51).

ATHLETICS: A WORD ABOUT HAZING

Hazing is behavior linked closely to the definition of bullying, which is repeated, intentional cruel acts between persons of unequal power. Hazing is also tied to a tradition or rituals of initiation that establish a hierarchy or pecking order within a team or other group. High school hazing often begins a week or two into the school year and is related to joining a team, club, or other group within the school.

These actions are often ritualistic in that they have occurred in past years to those who are now in the position of perpetuating the behavior on the new members. Additionally, these actions may require the target to participate in harmful and or humiliating practices. Sometimes these actions escalate over time and become more serious, humiliating, and dangerous. Tragically, some high school students have died from these rituals even when most states have made hazing against the law.

Media reports and research make reference to aggression being taught as acceptable behavior among athletes as a means of addressing conflict (Mintah, Huddleston, & Doody, 1999; Rowe, 1998). Rowe suggested that professional athletes model this aggressive behavior for youth athletes, exaggerating the problem: "Athletic development has proceeded at the expense of emotional development (and social development)." Contrary to the assertion that participation in sports may decrease aggressive behavior by redirecting it onto the playing field, Endresen and Olweus (2005) concluded that there is strong evidence that boys who participate in "power" or physical contact sports tend to be involved in violent and aggressive behavior outside of sports.

Nucci and Young-Shim (2005) discussed that unsportsmanlike behavior in young athletes can be a byproduct of the type of sport and the leadership of coaches within that sport. Athletes are better able to cope with potentially aggressive situations when they experience competition in sports in a healthy environment with quality leadership. Rowe (1998) reported that aggressive behavior in athletics can extend beyond the sport and into interpersonal relationships. Rhea and Lantz (2004) found that noncontact sport participants exhibited a significantly lower number of problematic behaviors (e.g., getting into trouble at school, assaulting others, and carrying weapons) than contact sport athletes or nonathletes.

Even though most athletes are aware of certain risks involved in athletics, they do not pursue sports involvement with the expectation of humiliation or degradation (Crow, Ammon, & Phillips, 2004). "Creating an environment in which hazing, bullying, and other forms of intimidation cannot thrive is the best way to ensure the safety and welfare of student-athletes" (Crow et al., 2004). Storch, Werner, and Storch (2003) found a correlation of relational aggression to poor peer relations and alcohol use among intercollegiate athletes.

This supports that programs aimed at reducing bullying and relational aggression implemented by coaches and others in leadership positions would serve to promote team cohesion. This book is designed to provide an offensive strategy striking the right balance from the view of the athletes, coaches, and fans to provide a bully-free athletic community and allow everyone to reap the benefits of sports and being part of a team.

2

WHY BULLYING PREVENTION?

It was easy for Jayden and Alex to call Pete gay. However, they found it was even more fun to get Jorge to do it because he had limited English. Jorge did not always realize when he was being used to make fun of or to humiliate someone else. In fact, he did not even realize he was being bullied when he was asked to stick his butt in someone's face in the locker room. One day when the coach heard about what had happened, Jorge got a strong warning and was told not to let it happen again.

Jorge felt good about having cool friends like Jayden and Alex and liked the attention he got from them for his antics with Pete. They had Jorge convinced that these kind of jokes were what teammates did to one another. A few days later Jayden, Alex, and Jorge found Pete in the locker room alone. Seizing on the opportunity and Jorge's vulnerability, Jayden and Alex told Jorge to stick his butt in Pete's face and call him gay. Jorge, although he didn't really want to, did as he was directed while Jayden and Alex watched, laughing hysterically.

Fortunately, the coach witnessed the entire incident and dealt with it. Jayden and Alex were given consequences according to the school bullying policy. The coach provided Jorge and Pete with guidance and opportunities to connect with other members of the team. The coach monitored them carefully so they would not be victimized again.

A major priority for athletic directors and coaches is the safety and well-being of their athletes. Established guidelines that describe acceptable behavior across all sports are both accepted and practiced by coaches, parents, and volunteers. For example, there are clear rules and guidelines for what to do when a storm comes up and lightning is near. All games and practices are immediately stopped and student athletes are placed in safe areas. There is even specialized equipment to alert us to the danger of lightning.

The intention of this book is to inspire creation and follow through with established guidelines to protect and assist in the development of the emotional and psychological well-being of our athletes. The hope and goals are that adults involved in youth athletics, regardless of whether they are volunteers or paid employees, will have the awareness and knowledge to recognize, prevent, and then intervene when bullying behavior occurs. Parents as partners in the athletic experience are not only to be aware of the issue of bullying, but need to know what to expect from any athletic program. Beyond that, everyone needs to understand that bullying occurs frequently in athletics with tremendous consequences. Most important, they need to know how to eliminate it.

We can demand excellence and personal best from athletes, but we must dispel the myth that demeaning and humiliating behaviors only strengthen and prepare our young athletes for "real life" by making them tough and strong. Likewise, we must dispel the myth that we can talk to athletes in their "own language" and use common profanity to reach these young people. We must dispel the myth that to be at the top you have to climb over others. Competition is about achievement and winning through personal best without crushing the dreams and hopes of others.

We need to dispel the myth that some athletes are more important than others. We can train and prepare winners on the field who understand and work together as a team. Positive experiences prepare members of a team to become socially responsible leaders with good character and ethics.

We must dispel the myth that fairness depends on the situation. Ethical behavior transcends all situations. There are no instances where it is okay not to be fair. After the whistle is blown, a hit in football or deliberately taking out the player guarding the base is neither fair nor ethical. When these behaviors are allowed or accepted they extend into other aspects of an athlete's life. There is a connection between these behaviors and bullying.

Young people cannot be expected to turn off their aggressive behavior after the game. Often that aggression comes out with peers, siblings, and toward themselves. Anger is a difficult and complex emotion and it often becomes aggression, which can be destructive and damaging. All these behaviors are not only related but also linked to bullying and can cause a climate of fear and mistrust.

Bullying is on the list of the greatest worries for our student athletes, just as it is for other students. It is not uncommon on our athletic field to hear comments from our student athletes about worries of being humiliated, embarrassed, or bullied. Friends are extremely important for young people. They are very concerned about their reputation with their peers and often lose faith in themselves as well as a sense of belonging when they have negative issues with their friends. Even though athletic teams are great avenues to build teamwork skills and self-esteem, there are times when they seem like battlefields for our kids. The fact of the matter is that bullying behavior happens in athletics but it does not get that label. In many instances, it is not only tolerated but also accepted.

Olweus (1994) found that bullying occurs not just once or twice but over and over again. Verbal bullying is the most common, and boys are more likely to be physically bullied. Nansel (2001) found that girls are more likely to report bullying, and approximately 30 percent of all children and youth in grades 6 through 10 have been bullied or have bullied someone else over a given semester.

According to Indicators of School Crime and Safety: 2008, in 2007, about a third (32 percent) of public and private school students ages 12–18 reported that they have been bullied at school within the past six months. Among high school students in grades 9–12, about 12 percent said they got into a fight on school property. In 2007, 10 percent of male students and 5 percent of female students reported experiencing a threat or injury with a weapon on school property. The percentage of students bullied at least once a week seems to have increased since 1999. Student bullying is one of the most frequently reported discipline problems at school: 21 percent of elementary schools, 43 percent of middle schools, and 22 percent of high schools

Some students struggle to understand the standards expected on the playing field. When adults as coaches, parents, and leaders of athletic programs scream at referees, coaches, and players with disrespect, kids get mixed messages of what constitutes appropriate behavior. Many adults understand the impact of this behavior. Yet others continue to believe that it teaches strength while others say that they are speaking in terms that kids will understand.

For many of our children today, a coach is a principle role model and provides teachings that last a lifetime. Many of our students have reported that there is a fine line between what motivates them and what makes them want to quit and give up on everything—including themselves. This standard applies to their relationship with adults as well as their peers. It often manifests in the form of relational aggression or emotional bullying. This can be the cruelest type of attack. The scars, although not visible, are often completely devastating.

The reality is that most, unfortunately, have experienced bullying at one time or another. As athletic leaders and coaches we can help break this vicious cycle. In order to prevent bullying behaviors we must take appropriate measures to stop bullying and help parents, athletes, and the community to recognize their role in prevention and their social responsibility.

The trust that is built between a coach and an athlete can provide the athlete who has been targeted an adult to go to for help. In addition, when athletes witness a coach coming to the rescue of somebody being targeted, they learn their role in prevention by supporting their peers on and off their team. The coach who leads bullying prevention efforts cultivates the ability to inspire others to action. This action can be seen in kids giving their full effort at practice and providing their best effort for the team, as well as commitment to core values and the code of conduct central to good sportsmanship.

We should never underestimate the value of good sportsmanship beyond the playing field. Confidence, tolerance, acceptance, courage, and humility are nurtured through sports and are great attributes in all aspects of a person's life. These are also most important when students are under pressure to exhibit behaviors that isolate, belittle, or torment peers. We can assist all athletes who witness unacceptable behaviors so they can stand up for others in a comfortable way. Athletes need to learn how to recognize what behaviors are unacceptable and what their role is in stopping and preventing them. Just imagine being in middle school witnessing bullying behaviors and not really knowing how to protect yourself from being the next target, let alone knowing what actions to take to protect others.

There is still a strong belief that to make a sports program successful and to build independent, strong, and successful children, we must teach them to be tough and prepare them for the harsh reality of life. This book will help you create student athletes who excel on and off the playing field and become the leaders of change in our schools who promote social responsibility and the bystander action necessary to reduce bullying in our schools. The necessary values may be taught through good sportsmanship and positive coaching. We can provide the environment that demands athletes to be their best, try their best, and promote the best in others.

We need to promote the concept of ethical behavior. We spend time discussing cheating, fair play, and health habits that are counterproductive to our bodies and athletic abilities, such as smoking and drinking. Bullying behavior that would never be allowed in the classroom cannot under any circumstances be allowed in the context of athletics. It is now time to promote moral and ethical behavior to also protect our athletes who exhibit bullying behaviors. Bullies often involve themselves in other risky behaviors and even criminal activity.

There are many myths that cause concern and hinder bullying prevention efforts. For example, fight back or become a bully yourself. The truth is that research supports that students who fight back are more likely to be continually victimized. Another myth that contributes to bullying behaviors is that we should allow children to resolve bullying themselves because children who bully will outgrow the behavior. The fact is that when we as adults do not intervene, we reinforce the behavior and the victim pays the price.

Even children who just witness bullying behaviors are at risk. This risk includes both long-term and short-term behaviors such as depression, isolation, and a loss of interest in school. Bullying affects everyone regardless of whether they are the victim, the perpetrator, or the bystander. To achieve a positive climate in our athletic programs we must put an end to the misconceptions that counteract bullying prevention efforts or cover them up.

Another myth says that physical bullying is much more serious than verbal and other forms of bullying. The fact is that name-calling and other verbal abuse can be equally and at times even more devastating than physical bullying. This form of bullying even takes place among friends and teammates. When it comes to sports, strengthening our children's character does not and should not involve any type of bullying behaviors. Bullying tactics do not toughen up our kids. On the contrary, they work against helping them achieve in their academics, athletics, and overall emotional well-being.

Research has shown that children who bully tend to have more positive attitudes toward violence, are easily frustrated, have difficulty conforming to rules, are stronger than their peers, and show very little compassion for children they victimized. Research has indicated that many children who bully have high self-esteem, debunking the myth that students use bullying behaviors because they have low self-esteem and want to feel better about themselves.

When it comes to athletics we need to be realistic that the athletic arena is challenging and difficult enough without the negative effects of bullying added to the roster. When bullying enters the arena it can be devastating to the victim, bystanders, and athletic culture. The suffering can be internalized and lead students to drop out of sports. We must be realistic about the types of bullying that occur in all athletic programs. It is foolish to believe that all coaches and athletic staff understand the signs and symptoms of bullying and that the strategies to intervene and deal with it can be handled in a casual way. We must understand that bullying behaviors unchecked can become an accepted part of the culture.

Most important, we must embrace our role in athletics to prevent bullying and provide a positive athletic environment that builds athletes who excel in their sport, sportsmanship, and overall good character. Solving bullying problems can be accomplished through reporting incidents, acknowledging and coming to the aid of victims, singling out and correcting bullying behaviors, and having fair and consistent consequences. Protect our athletes and our athletic programs from deliberate indifference by weeding out the bullies and bullying behavior.

Through athletics, there are great opportunities to teach and model social responsibility and the best ways to treat each other. We have learned what needs to be done across society to help foster the type of behaviors that combat bullying. Our actions, rules, and policies must provide clarity and consistency of expectations in the code of conduct. This begins with a clear understanding of bullying behavior and then a comprehensible plan to eliminate it.

TEN KEY FACTS REGARDING BULLYING IN ATHLETICS

1. Bullying usually occurs where there is minimal adult supervision, such as certain times in the locker room, bathrooms, on the Internet, and at unchaperoned social events.

Bullying can be very subtle and subversive, and it can happen anywhere. However, clearly, bullying can be reduced if there is more supervision. Bullying can happen whenever there is a gathering of kids, as at athletic events. Research from the National Center for Educational Statistics found that "bullying appears to take place more in middle or junior high schools rather than in high schools" (Nolin, Davies, & Chandler, 1995).

When dealing with athletes, coaches or other supervisors should try to have a presence in the areas where they gather. Having an adult around minimizes bullying behaviors under unofficial circumstances as well as official ones. It is important to have proper supervision for practices and events. Bullying prevention is a team effort and everyone needs to do their part for it to be successful. Bullying happens when adults allow it, ignoring it and denying that it is occurring. Our adult presence and impact on the social culture can create or prevent an environment that fosters bullying behaviors. Our athletes are very impressionable and the coach can be a powerful and effective influence that deters bullying.

2. Hazing and bullying in athletics occurs in all forms—physical, verbal, and relational.

Bullying can happen in many different ways. It can be physical—hitting, pushing, and the other common means identified with bullying. In addition, bullying in athletics can happen when certain members of the team single out other members to perform menial tasks. For instance, the practice of the captains of the varsity track team who order the same group of freshmen to haul out the mats and equipment to the field can be bullying.

Many practices, while not exactly hazing, are directed specifically at certain team members. Hazing refers to any activity expected of someone joining a group (or to maintain full status in a group) that humiliates, degrades, or risks emotional or physical harm, regardless of the person's willingness to participate (Nuwer, 2000). As children grow and develop, their peer group and social inclusion become one of the most important issues for them. Sports participation and being a part of a team often provide a peer group that becomes central to the athlete. When the team rejects, excludes, or humiliates another team member, the effect can be devastating.

Any form of bullying can impact the team and athletes should be held accountable for the actions on and off the field with their teammates and all peers for that matter. The coach has the power to tackle bullying by early prevention and education about the various forms of bullying. The coach becomes the change agent of the culture that condones these behaviors by a lack of action or ignoring their existence to one that manages the behaviors and sets the tone for acceptable treatment of others.

3. Bullying behaviors are detrimental to the benefits of participating in athletics.

It is all about character, character, and more character—or that is the common thread of all programs geared toward developing good sportsmanship in young athletes. John Wooden, the great college basketball coach, said, "Ability may get you on top but it takes character to keep you there."

Treating others, including team members, with respect is essential to developing the precise skills most coaches strive to develop in their athletes. Respect is at the core of bullying prevention. When there is an absence of respect, for whatever reason, the general atmosphere is impacted by bullying behavior. When bullying is allowed, automatically there is a lack of trust and confidence overshadowing the team. When the team loses trust and confidence, the immediate result is the breaking down of teamwork and respect for one another.

We shouldn't deny that bullying behaviors can infiltrate any environment and close our eyes to the bullying that does happen every day in our schools, playgrounds, and playing fields. Rather, we should understand that coaches are the ultimate teachers of character and respect and provide the foundation for building a good climate that goes beyond the sport and carries into the school and everyday fabric of the athletes they coach. Understanding the key role coaches and other adults play in building character and fostering respect in our youth is critical to bullying prevention.

4. Many coaches are not provided with bullying prevention training as other educators and caretakers are.

Good sportsmanship is the common goal for coaches. But there seems to be confusion about the application of that concept. Few programs address bullying prevention as part of the coaches' training. For example, while the expectation is that athletes will shake hands when the competition is over, this is only as good as its enforcement. Some coaches verbally abuse some athletes as a method to improve athletic performance. There was a time in the 1970s when this type of behavior management for athletes was used by the Soviet Union to motivate athletes for the Olympics. At that time it was considered to be a state-of-the-art approach to developing athletes.

Today for many, it is passé to think that threats, humiliation, extreme exhaustion, deprivation, fear, guilt, or shame could possibly motivate an athlete to be successful. Yet often shouting and humiliation are still considered motivators. This has been seen as a way to make athletes strong and tough (Schinnerer, 2009). This is bullying and we know from experience that it can have lasting negative effects on young people. Bullying prevention needs to be an integral part of training for coaches. Proper training is essential to developing good sportsmanship, good athletes, commitment, and pride in one's team.

Team building occurs in an atmosphere of respect, consideration, connection, and commitment to one goal. When there is trust, caring, and a shared physical experience, not only will kids learn but they will also bond in a way that unites them as a team. They need to believe that the coach not only knows them but also truly cares about them not only as a team but also as individuals.

5. Physical aggression is somewhat more prevalent in boys than girls, but both girls and boys are involved in all forms of bullying.

Gender plays a part in the type of bullying that happens among children. Boys have been associated with physical bullying and girls have been known for nonphysical aggression.

In athletics, athletes who don't do well are commonly called gay or other sexual orientation comments used in a derogatory way by coaches, athletes, and just about everyone else. The 2007 National School Climate Survey conducted by GLSEN (Gay, Lesbian and Straight Education Network) states: Keeping classrooms and hallways free of homophobic, sexist and other types of biased language is a crucial aspect of creating a safe school climate for students. Yet research tells us 9 out of 10 lesbian, gay, bisexual, and transgender students hear sexual orientation remarks made in their schools every day.

If you just listen to the daily language of people in general, you will hear comments that are related to gender and sexuality on a regular basis. Some educators believe that it is so common that kids do not even know they are using hurtful language. By repeatedly using these terms, the tone of disrespect for differences in sexual orientation becomes accepted and part of the culture. But to any student who has been humiliated by these labels it is painful.

In the athletic arena—an atmosphere that is identified with power, strength, and toughness—weakness is often described in terms related to sexual orientation. In other words, the opposite of being tough is to be weak and act "like a girl" or a "homo." It can even include calling a boy "Miss" or a group of boys "girls." These expressions and many more of this nature are used regularly on the playing field. Whether it is boys or girls involved in bullying behaviors, in their mind they assume it will make them popular. Kids have consistently reported that they bully others because they get "respect" from their peers. This is a form of social power and should be recognized as unacceptable.

One common form of bullying is relational. This type of bullying can be devastating. Research shows that 61 percent of adolescents say that they have experienced relational aggression at least once in the last month (Sullivan, Farrell, & Kliewer, 2006). Relational aggression that is intended to purposely prevent or disrupt relationships among individuals includes but is not limited to withholding friendship, ignoring others, spreading rumors, gossiping, and eliciting peer rejection of another child (Crick, 1995). This is by no means a complete list of the ways in which relational bullying can occur, but it is meant to show that bullying is much more than physical. It also does not necessarily suggest that girls are the only ones who use relational aggression. However, research supports that boys use more direct physical means and girls tend to use more underhanded, relational forms of aggression to frustrate and interrupt the social goals of other girls.

> 6. Bullying occurs in athletes of all ages and all levels from recreational sports to the professional leagues.

Bullying happens at every age unless it is stopped. In fact it can be seen on the youth fields as well as the professional level. The important thing to remember is that the sooner there is an intervention, the less likely it is to continue. In the early years, not only will bullying that goes unchecked continue, but others will adopt the behavior as well. When kids see the behavior as a means to exercise power over another, they are more likely to do the same. Athletics is about the development of personal, physical, and athletic power, so it makes sense that this is an area where bullying can be confused with preparing kids to be strong and tough.

At the middle school level, bullying is related to social status and positioning in a group. When bullying goes unchecked at this age, peer aggression increases (Juvonen, 2007). This age is most difficult because of the children's physical and emotional development stages. Social connection is most important at this age. Team sports can be a place where young people make connections that will carry them through these turbulent years. However, if bullying is allowed or encouraged, it can have long-term effects on students.

Unless there is a prevention program in place, bullying occurs at the high school level also. It is interesting to note that at this point athletes do not recognize bullying as a problem. If you talk to them, they will say it does not happen in their school. But further observation and questions reveal that it happens in many varied and subtle ways. Some of these behaviors can include exclusion of one or more by the other members of the team. They can include other forms of humiliation. In any case it is important to note that when bullying goes unchecked at the earlier levels, it just continues and escalates. When students are older, bullying behaviors can become more serious and damaging, and may be against the law.

Athletes who bully are often leaders in the school. They will bully their peers to dominate and control them. They choose this behavior because they use their power to gain social status and popularity within their peer group. Often these individuals have more leeway to commit these bullying behaviors because of their status as athletes. It happens more often than not that athletes are less likely to get in trouble, particularly when their sport is in season. The common term for those instances is "athletic privilege."

> 7. Many students do not report incidents of bullying for fear of retaliation.

When bullying occurs, athletes are reluctant to report it to anyone. Fear of retaliation is a real issue for all kids. However, for athletes it is even more pronounced due to their strong sense of loyalty to the team. In other words, teams need to be loyal and protective of their members. They are taught to rely on one another and to be proud of their affiliation to the team. It is very serious to breach that trust and very few athletes are willing to do it. We should not, as coaches and so on, put our kids in this position.

This is the point where support from adults becomes essential to protect athletes who are willing to step forward and speak up. Retaliation can be direct: hurtful revenge from the person who was causing the problem. Or it can be indirect: other members of the team are vengeful toward the athlete who reported the bullying.

Adults need to make basic values and expectations clear to the athletes. The rules need to be set with clear consequences. They also need to know that those rules are upheld consistently and applied to everyone—no matter who they are or what part of the season it is (i.e., no exceptions for athletes just before a game or meet).

Also, if there is any retaliation, it needs to be dealt with immediately and firmly, just like the grade policy on athletic participation. To allow this behavior to continue undermines the purpose of the rules and upsets the climate of the team. Kids need to trust and that begins with the adults that are in charge to guarantee that they feel safe.

8. Parents may be the perpetrators of bullying behaviors toward athletes.

There are many ways that parents can bully athletes, coaches, and even game officials. Extreme spectator booing will impact the performance of athletes, as research clearly indicates. While it is considered a home team advantage, it can actually influence the concentration, performance, and attitude of the athletes. It has also been shown to influence the game officials' rulings. In other words, a bad call can elicit booing from the crowd that then can influence future decisions, causing further crowd reaction (Greer, 1983). Bullying behaviors may be reinforced or encouraged by this type of inappropriate behavior.

We are not by any means suggesting that the crowd should not be in the game. It is exciting to be a spectator and support your team. However, there is a difference between supporting your team and shouting profanity, booing, and throwing things onto the field. Parents often argue and disagree with each other in a bullying manner. Spectators need to distinguish between the two behaviors. Programs have been created with rules for spectators and in some instances parents are required to sign a contract that outlines appropriate behavior expectations for all parents and spectators.

When spectators exhibit behaviors that shame or humiliate others, they are serving to spark bullying behaviors in our athletes who observe their behaviors. When other spectators do not address the inappropriate behaviors of these spectators, they are encouraging the behaviors through their silence. As we discuss later in the book, bystanders are a crucial ingredient to tackling bullying in athletics.

9. Good sportsmanship must be modeled, taught, and reinforced.

Good sportsmanship is much more than the common platitude if it is not based in character education. It needs to be at the center of any program that is implemented with fidelity across all the practices and expectations of the team. Training for good sportsmanship needs to include professional development for all the staff involved in the athletic program. It has to go across the board and reflect the programs and policies of the school or community at large. But above all, behaviors that demonstrate good sportsmanship need to be modeled and practiced in every aspect of the program.

Good sportsmanship is one of the main benefits athletes gain from sports participation. We, as coaches and role models, need to help our athletes see the link between good sportsmanship and a successful season. For our kids to buy into the concept of good sportsmanship we must make educating and reinforcing their sportsmanship a priority with specific actions. When poor sportsmanship is exhibited, there must be policies and procedures to address it. Promoting good sportsmanship involves clear rules, cultivating behaviors over time and consequences when good sportsmanship is not displayed. In this book we discuss the elements of good sportsmanship and how they can be used to prevent bullying.

10. Bullying laws, rules, and policies must be enforced on and off the playing field and in the virtual world.

All rules, policies, and laws related to bullying need to be consistent and everyone needs to understand and agree that bullying prevention is essential to the safety, well-being, and success of the team. There must be a clear understanding that these rules apply both on and off the playing field, including the cyberworld. The culture of the athletic department must support the rules and policies and send the message that there is no room for bullying in athletics. When bullying behaviors occur, coach intervention must occur immediately to stop the behavior and ensure there are no repercussions or retaliation for anyone involved in the incident.

Our athletes are part of the Net generation, who prefer texting and other virtual means of communicating rather than face to face. This may lead to a blurring of what is virtual and what is "real." Our athletes, like most kids in this Net generation, are exposed to violent behaviors through the Internet and video games that are accessible almost anytime and anywhere. Cell phones are mini computers that provide access to the virtual world for a relatively low monthly fee. In addition, instant replays are not just for the referees, judges, and coaches. Video and photo features allow athletes to capture embarrassing moments and share them with an entire school community for an indefinite length of time. Cyberbullying must be addressed to tackle bullying even in athletics.

3

ATHLETES: THE VIEW FROM THE PLAYING FIELD

Jeanne was a very popular cheerleader. She had been taking gymnastics and cheering since she was nine years old. She was very good at developing new and innovative choreography. Like her teammates, she loved the attention and prestige that came from wearing her uniform on game day. But when it came time to vote for captain, Bethany got the most votes. Jeanne was devastated. She had been waiting and planning for this for as long as she could remember and now she had been outvoted by another girl.

Jeanne was so angry, feeling that she was robbed of the title of captain, that she started a blog to vent her feelings. The blog grew into a place for others to talk about Bethany. It went well beyond Jeanne's intention of venting her feelings about not making captain and became a Bethany hate club. At practices, members of the squad would laugh at the inside jokes that were discussed on the blog. It was confusing for Bethany because she did not understand how a squad of cheerleaders who supported her by voting her captain could so suddenly turn on her.

When she found out about the blog, Bethany was humiliated. She tried to ignore it but references from the blog were everywhere. The whole school seemed to be laughing at her expense. Even when she was at home and trying not to think about it, her friends would send her texts and e-mails with up-to-date postings and comments bashing her. When she walked down the hallway at school, other students would stare at her and laugh as she went by. She eventually quit the squad.

KICKOFF: WHY PLAY SPORTS?

Children choose to participate in sports for many reasons. Basically kids participate in sports because it is fun. Belonging to a group is very important to kids and participation in sports gives them a sense of belonging. This is the key to social acceptance. Wearing that team jersey to school on game day and associating with teammates is very important to kids as they are growing and developing their social identity. The team gives them a group focused on similar interests.

Automatically when they join a team, kids can feel a sense of belonging. Many times kids will join a team because their friends are playing that sport. This also is an opportunity to make new friends. The friends that they make in the context of a team sport are special. It is about a particular sense of camaraderie, working together toward a common goal. While team practice is considered work, kids have the sense of belonging and being a part of something that is important to them and, of course, that gives them the chance of becoming a winner.

Kids play sports because they like the action and excitement of them. Most kids would rather participate than sit on the sidelines or the bench. They like the idea of being needed and feeling important.

As they work at practice and participate in games or meets, bonds are formed. Athletes have built-in support from their friends. It is a type of alliance that fosters a social solidarity. In other words, kids can feel part of something that helps to define who they are and to develop a sense of connection. It is this sense of connection that gives kids confidence when they go into the larger school population. This is positive peer acceptance and it is very important to preadolescents and adolescents as they grow socially and emotionally.

The image of being with a team as a member is also very important. It becomes a part of the student's identity. It is through that identity that the student feels a sense of belonging and a part of the school community. Certainly there are other avenues within a school that can give a student the same feelings. This can include, for instance, student government—but often the class officers and other organizers of the school are athletes. There seems to be a connection between participation in athletics, popularity, and leadership.

As members of a team, kids learn how to work as part of a group. They learn that winning is a team effort and as individuals they are part of a team with a single goal. Team members care about one another and they have solidarity. Their actions directly impact everyone. That is a very important life lesson for young people to learn and a very important key to developing a bully-free environment. When kids look out for one another, bullying is less likely to occur. The team environment is a natural setting to teach these values.

Other reasons that kids decide to take part in a sport include the desire to develop their physical attributes and the skills related to the sport that they choose. Throwing, passing, hitting, swimming, and skating are just a few of the variety of physical skills that are cultivated when a student is part of a team. In other words, what better way to develop a love for a sport than by participating as a member of a team?

It is important to mention that kids have the right to refuse to play any sport. It is for them to choose. Of course it's okay to encourage your child to play, but it's not okay to pressure her or him. The difficulty lies in the ability of the adult to distinguish between encouragement and pressure. Parents need to be very careful that they don't push their own goals onto their child so hard that involvement in sports becomes stressful instead of pleasurable. Of course it is important to encourage children to participate in sports at any level, but only if they want to. Once involved in sports, the parent's support, encouragement, and approval adds to the pleasure a youth gets from participating in a sport.

There are many reasons why kids choose to quit participating in a sport, which can be as simple as losing interest or developing an interest in some nonsport activity. Time can also be a factor in why children may choose to drop a sport. As they get older, their academic demands grow and also their social life becomes more important.

To the athlete, the view from the playing field is not always one of inspiration. When the whistle blows to start a game or practice it often triggers nervousness, worry, and anxiety. The student may choose to quit because of pressure from parents or coaches. The training may be intense—beyond their physical and developmental capabilities. This is a certain turnoff for the kid who wanted to participate for fun and affiliation with peers. Ultimately, children mostly leave sports if they feel inadequate or really not good enough to participate.

Parental support is crucial for kids to remain enthusiastic and committed to the sport. This means that the child needs the appropriate equipment and uniforms. For the athlete it is important that whatever the appropriate equipment may be for their particular sport, it should be easy to use, comfortable, and hassle-free.

Uniforms are an important component of the athletic experience for kids. Whether it is a T-shirt or entire uniform, it solidifies the connection and identification with the team. For the athlete it is a symbol of prestige and status among their peers. You can see the Little League or soccer T-shirts in elementary school and varsity shirts in high school hallways. In other words, kids are proud of their sport and love to wear their uniforms at any age and feel the connection of belonging to a group or team.

This is central to why students play sports. As children grow and develop socially, identification with peers is central to their own feelings of self-worth. They can identify with their teammates and feel connected to a sport that helps them to define themselves. This can be very important for social development, as well as physical attributes.

According to the *American Heritage Dictionary*, the term *team* means "joining together on the same side." Athletes take this notion very seriously. From their perspective the team is more important than the individual. They work, practice, and play together with a focus on teamwork, and with that comes friendship and camaraderie. They share both the wins and losses as a team unit, which helps them to form strong solid bonds with each other. Therefore, when it comes to bullying prevention, team loyalty must be discussed, defined, and monitored to assure all teammates of their value.

There are times when team loyalty can be detrimental and entice bullying behavior. This bullying may come from peers on the team. Often when bullying involves another team member it is allowed to continue because speaking up or reporting it could potentially impact the entire team. Research by Ojala and Nesdale (2004) looked at the connection between bullying and social identity. In the study they looked at the responses of kids to stories that involved bullying and helpful behaviors. When the story was about members of the "in group," the behavior was acceptable. On the other hand the same actions when committed by the "unpopular" group were unacceptable. This is important to consider because from the point of view of the athlete, bullying behavior is more acceptable members of their own group are doing it. The social identity of the athletic team is powerful. From the perspective of the athlete, it is important to foster a social identity that includes rejecting all bullying behaviors.

It is very difficult for athletes to speak up because they would not want to break the bonds of team loyalty or get a fellow teammate in trouble. This can be a great stress for these children regardless of whether they are the one being victimized or the bystander. The better athletes tend to bully the ones that are not so gifted.

The link of bullying and school violence must bring our attention to the violence on the playing field. There is an increasing concern regarding violence among children and youth on our playgrounds and athletic fields. In the last decade, violence by and against children and adolescents has received media attention, public concern, and research. Community violence is reflected in our organized sports and this behavior must be curbed through awareness, education, and action. Participating in sports provides valuable physical, academic, emotional, and health opportunities for our youth. However, too often these athletic activities may actually support violence with a bully culture.

HALFTIME: RELATIONSHIP WITH THE COACH

Coaches, just like most teachers, often feel that their methods of motivating kids and providing a respectful environment conducive to learning is pretty effective. However, they often get frustrated when they have to address certain behavioral issues. Effective educators, on and off the playing field, need the skills and training to teach youths how to minimize certain negative behaviors. Coaches want to feel as comfortable assessing certain behaviors as they do athletic achievement. Social behaviors may be out of their sphere of reference. This is often true with classroom teachers; they feel much more comfortable assessing academic achievement than nonacademic issues, but they must do both.

It is crucial for coaches to realize that the relationship they have with their athletes may contribute to certain unacceptable behaviors unintentionally. When bullying behaviors are not addressed, the bully believes he or she has the coach's approval.

For many of our young players, the coach becomes someone they can talk to about any issues or concerns. We should encourage all athletes to report incidents of bullying and tell someone if they believe they may be being bullied. The coach and often the team can and should serve as a go-to place when they are in trouble. In regard to bullying, any participation as a victim, perpetrator, or bystander is nothing but trouble. When students feel comfortable reporting bullying behaviors, we are on the right track to preventing bullying in athletics.

It is discouraging for parents to know that their children dread sports that they used to love. Additionally, parents feel bad to hear that a child wants to quit and feels sick at the thought of a game or practice. Too often children comment on another teammate's performance by saying, "Thanks for making us lose" or "You suck," which makes them want out. Team loyalty and respect have turned into verbal and even psychological abuse. The sad reality is that this doesn't just come from peers alone. Coaches and other adults often use words in the guise of motivation that instead tear down an athlete's self-esteem and minimize or eliminate the benefits of sports. John Schinnerer (2009) noted in his work that verbal and emotional abuse is much more common in athletics than anywhere else. It can lead to severe and long-lasting negative effects on the athlete's social and emotional development.

Coaching involving humiliation does not serve a purpose in sports, is not effective, and can cause long-term damage. Coaches that use disparaging words are not limited to a specific sport or gender. We are seeing this type of "coaching" from Little League to the big leagues. We must provide role models who can be demanding without being demeaning and who can disagree without being disagreeable. When players are humiliated and their dedication, talent, and loyalty are constantly challenged they may decide to end their involvement in sports.

Coaches need to be able to create an opportunity to evaluate the athletes' skills in a way that is constructive and teaches the necessary skills for the athlete to grow and to meet attainable goals mentally and physically. All of this needs to happen with a clear understanding of the athlete's skill level. In other words, the focus needs to be on positive constructive criticism without belittling the athlete.

There are simple ways that we can teach athletes—and everyone for that matter—to help a victim:

- Ask the victim if he or she is okay. Ask or tell the bully to stop it. Verify that the victim is okay and is actually being bullied and simply tell the bully to stop it.
- If the victim is not okay, get an adult immediately to help.
- Remove the victim from the incident and walk away with the victim. Groups or witnesses reinforce a culture that supports bullying behavior—walking away with the victim removes him or her from the situation.
- If you are afraid of retaliation, get an adult to intervene. Do not put yourself at risk. bullying is about victimization and sometimes it takes an adult to stop it.

POSTGAME: ROLE MODELS IMPACTING THE FUTURE

Role models that promote athletes reaching their athletic potential without insulting and belittling set the tone for how teammates treat each other. Young people learn how to behave by the adult behavior they see. Adults who cannot coach children in a culture guided by respect should not be coaches. Currently, sports participation holds a value beyond the playing field as it provides opportunities for growth in leadership, collaboration, determination, and responsibility. If we don't provide the right leadership skills to those who hold our sports leadership positions, we may get unintended negative outcomes from our athletes. These unintended outcomes, mainly bullying, will then carry into our schools and community. Therefore it is in the best interest of adults, parents, and coaches to remember that their actions as well as their comments all affect our athletes. So whatever you say, think carefully on how to say it and use your body language carefully as well. Remember, actions speak louder than words.

Our student athletes need coaches with standards of personal integrity and honesty. Coaches must recognize that they are role models to players. Coaches must set the example of the behavior they want to see in their players. Like any other teachers, coaches must have a presence that both gives and deserves respect. The saying, "Do as I say, not as I do" will never work in prevention efforts.

Our players must learn to trust the adults around them. They must feel confident that they may go to a coach for assistance if they are on the receiving end of bullying behaviors. In turn, parents should be able to trust that coaches will identify and intervene if bullying incidents occur. Athletes who feel uncomfortable or threatened should feel comfortable going to their coach, and know that the coach will address the situation in a positive way and put an end to it.

Our athletes need to know that someone else's behavior should not make them feel threatened or uncomfortable. Athletes should be in an environment where everyone has the right to be and is respected. When circumstances arise that compromise this environment something will be done to correct it.

Several members of a golf team took turns hiding items of another player who never participated in bullying behaviors. One game day they stuck his golf shoes in a dirty toilet. This is clearly bullying. The receptiveness, imbalance of power, and the intent to be hurtful are there. It is certain that the athlete being victimized was bothered by the acts. Unfortunately, not every case is as easy to recognize when bullying is occurring. In later chapters, we help with considerations that will help coaches, parents, and other athletes recognize bullying behaviors, which come in many forms.

When considering the view from the playing field we must realize that athletes are not immune from victimization or exhibiting bullying. Our athletes witness their peers getting made fun of each and every day. For our athletes, any athletic achievement or failure could place them in situations to be subjected to derogatory names and bullying behaviors. Teammates and "friends" may join in the behaviors in their desire to fit in at all costs. Being too strong, too tall, too awkward, too fast, or too slow could trigger victimization. It is quite challenging to determine how and why certain athletes are viewed differently by peers and fellow players.

The bottom line is athletes are not immune to bullying. The good news is that the rules of the sport and foundation of sportsmanship help minimize bullying and the idea that athletes have special privileges and rules in schools and athletic departments. The myth that those that exhibit bullying behaviors are strong and fit the stereotypes of athletes will disappear. As student athletes will tell us, size and stature are not requirements to use bullying behaviors online, as many athletes have experienced cyberbullying.

Before we ask bystanders to be proactive, we have to talk to them about how they can respond, act, or proceed to get help (see figure 3.1). For example, to help someone who is being bullied, a student athlete may do the following things.

Walk Away

For the victim, one way to handle a potentially difficult situation is to simply walk away. This may be difficult as it often requires tremendous self-discipline not to respond. Traditionally in the context of sports, striking back is an integral part of what athletes are taught. In most sports, coaches teach and even demand toughness and quick response to adversity on the playing field. This is an important part of competition so it is contradictory to ask an athlete to choose to walk away from a bullying situation.

We need to help athletes understand that in these situations, walking away takes greater courage than risking victimization. Bullying is not about rising to the challenge of competition between equals; rather it is about victimization on an unequal playing field. Walking away will

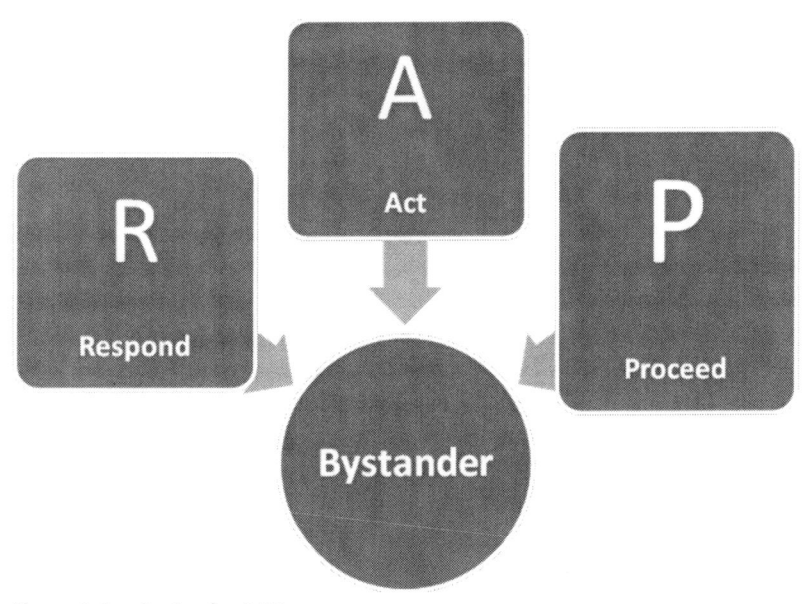

Figure 3.1. Bystander RAP

often diffuse the situation. Therefore walking away can be a very safe alternative to interrupting a bullying behavior.

Walking away can be very effective when bystanders are involved. It can be as simple as saying, "Why don't you come with us?" Brief and straightforward comments can be very effective because they send a powerful message from the bystander. Since most bullying happens when there is an audience, when a bystander intervenes it shifts the focus. The person who is bullying no longer has peer support and encouragement to continue the behavior; it is less likely to continue.

Tell an Adult

It is very important for adults to be made aware of bullying situations. However, it can be difficult to bring these reports to an adult because it appears to be a sign of weakness. Bullying happens when someone is unable to protect himself. As adults we are responsible for the safety of those in our care, so it is imperative that adults respond quickly and appropriately when we hear about a bullying incident.

When those reports are made, bystanders need to know that the situation has been handled and they will be protected from retaliation. They need to be supported and praised for their courage to stand up for someone who is vulnerable.

Step In

Intervening is the most obvious tool to stop bullying behavior. It may take little more than a few words. It can be as simple as saying, "Come on, leave him alone," or "Hey there, let's get out of here." Sometimes that is all it takes to interrupt a process that, if ignored, can get out of hand.

Stepping in can work well when there is a group of bystanders who all together reject the bullying behavior. It is in numbers that students are most safe from the backlash of any bullying incident.

Use Humor

Humor has always been a great way to relieve a tense situation. This needs to be done in a way that will not escalate the situation. And of course the humor needs to be respectful. After all, insulting someone in return for bullying behavior only makes the situation worse. However, making light of a situation can be a very good option for bystanders and victims. Humor can diffuse the focus on the victim and involve bystanders.

Talk to the Victim

Perceptions are very important, so it makes sense to check in with the victim to be certain that bullying is really occurring. The line between teasing and bullying can be difficult to figure out and most of the time it is the victim that makes that call. So asking if it is okay—"Are you good with what they are saying to you?"—can give the victim an opportunity to talk. This can let victims know that they are not alone and that they have an ally—someone they can rely on should the bullying continue or even get worse.

Talking to the victim can help the situation particularly when there is an imbalance of power. Often the one who is victimized is further rejected by his peers for fear they will be victimized as well. Bullies often have many supporters. Having an ally levels the playing field for the victim.

Tell Their Friends

Making good friends and staying with them in pairs, groups, and clusters is an excellent way to avoid bullying situations. Bullying most often happens when the group focuses on one or two students. When the numbers are equal or the victim is not alone, it is less likely to occur. Talking to friends raises awareness and helps set up safe situations. Friends are often willing to help because they know that when in a group they are less likely to become the victim themselves.

Be Assertive

Sometimes speaking up is a valid way to protect oneself from bullying. However, if the target is comfortable enough to speak up, it may not be a true bullying incident because there may not be an imbalance of power. But certainly we are looking to have students solve issues as simply and as soon as they arise. So it makes sense to have being assertive as a first line of defense—when they feel safe enough to do it. Statements like "We are a team and we have to work together" or simply "Leave me alone" can stop bullying behavior.

According to the research of Craig and Pepler (1997), many peer bystanders do not intervene because children may not know the expectations of adults. This solidifies the need for all the adults in an athlete's life need to be clear about expectations when it comes to bullying behavior. We need to support bystanders when they report bullying behavior. They need to know that you will listen and they will want to see you respond in a way that protects them as well as the victim.

In addition, there is a level of courage necessary to stand up to someone who is bullying someone else. We can and should empower athletes to intervene in a way that is safe and comfortable. However, we need to understand that they may find standing up for others a difficult thing to do. Just as an adult would need to consider the personal consequences and the safety of jumping into a situation with our peers, we need to understand that for athletes it is the same. By giving easy and safe examples we can and should help athletes take a stand against bulling behaviors.

Not every incident warrants peer intervention. It is essential to help athletes understand the options for intervention and when it is best to seek an adult rather than try to intervene. In some cases, simply saying stop or knock it off will work, but at other times they could be vulnerable to retaliation and further victimization. There is a tendency in groups of athletes or students for the crowd to diffuse responsibility when bullying occurs.

We must help stop the thinking that someone else will or should be helping out. We must remove the tendency to think, "It's not my problem." It can be that any one of the bystanders as an individual would never stand for the bullying behavior, but in a group they begin to feel that if no one is speaking up, why should they? The accountability to stop the behavior is shifted to the group as a whole.

In addition, bystanders begin to lose empathy for the victim. They begin to think that the victim actually likes it. How many times have we heard, "Oh, he likes it when we do that" or "We do that all the time"?

Retaliation is very real and a powerful deterrent for a potential bystander to act. It is so very important for there to be an adult support system and a clear set of rules against bullying behavior to alleviate this fear. Once athletes and all kids see there is action and consequences for bullying behavior, it will most certainly decrease.

Keeping that in mind, we need to strive to empower those looking to intervene responsibly or seek help immediately. Many athletes and all kids in general may not have the skills to intervene when bullying occurs.

A simple way to look at bullying in the athletic arena is to think JOCK:

- J: Jump in.
- O: Offer help.
- C: Call for assistance.
- K: Keep on your guard so it will not happen again.

Catchy sayings like this can help athletes remember ways to stop bullying behavior. JOCK or the Bystander RAP are tools that can be used to remind everyone involved about the expectations that relate not only to building a strong team but how to be great role models for the entire school population. These sayings can be used on bullying prevention posters in the locker room and anywhere teams meet. The posters can be part of presenting a positive image of the team. They reinforce that bullying behavior is not acceptable and that good sportsmanship and team success begins with standing up for each other and treating everyone with respect.

4

COACHES: THE VIEW FROM THE LOCKER ROOM

STORIES FROM THE SIDELINES

When it came to the attention of the superintendent of schools, it already was a big problem. It seems that a group of athletes attacked a teammate in the locker-room showers. They contended that it was all in fun—"You know, we were just playing with the towels and we were snapping them at each other." They said that it was a thing that happens all the time and in fact we all had similar experiences when we were freshmen.

However, the parents of the victim were very concerned about the serious welts and black and blue bruises he had all over his lower body. To them this was well beyond good fun or some type of joke. In fact, despite Michael's protests, they sought medical attention for the wounds and reported the incident to the school.

Athletes may horse around in a locker room and often these behaviors are unsupervised and go unaddressed. There is a fine line between just playing around and bullying behaviors. Proper supervision and a culture of respect prevent these types of behaviors from escalating to bullying.

When the superintendent called the coach for an explanation, he supported the story that it was all in fun and a sort of tradition that the older varsity did to welcome new team members. Furthermore, the coach stated that as an adult, it was not appropriate for him to be present in the shower with adolescent boys. The superintendent instructed the coach to develop a procedure for adult supervision of athletes at all times and places, including the locker room and showers.

Clearly this is a situation that could have been avoided if the coach had a procedure that included supervision and a personal approach with the students that fostered respect. The clue to this problem is that the coach did not take the issue seriously and therefore it escalated to the level of the superintendent. Coaches are role models and by accepting any negative behavior they are actually supporting or condoning that behavior, which will not only continue but will also surely escalate.

Coaches need regular evaluation and feedback that can be utilized for improvement in building relationships with students that foster respect. Coaches want feedback so they can do a good job and measure particular strengths and weaknesses to analyze actions for improvement, harness the good things, and modify behaviors that are less effective. Honest evaluation of their interpersonal skills, including communication, motivation, and supervision, is an effective tool to build the culture of a team and athletic program.

KICKOFF: COACHES DEFINE THE CULTURE OF ATHLETIC PROGRAMS

Coaches are role models, mentors, professionals, authorities, and teachers that play an important role in influencing their athletes. Very often success only arrives with winning and it is difficult to balance praising athletes for great effort, improvement in skills, and teamwork when the outcome is defeat. There is certainly nothing wrong with wanting to win. In fact, we should enter every sport with the intention to do the best we possibly can and win. The problem facing many coaches is how to motivate and correct shortcomings while being positive and avoiding being negative. Coaches have expertise in their sport but not necessarily in working with children and teenagers. Teachers placed in a classroom with subject matter expertise without knowledge of pedagogy would probably not provide the learning environment necessary to have students reach their potential, just like coaches without the proper training in working with children and teens. Clear distictions between anger, fear, conflict, and bullying have not been made clear to coaches and athletes.

Many times the road to defeat is paved with the best intentions. There are practices coaches use truly believing they are acting in the best interest of the athletes they coach when they are actually working against their best interest. Competition is often confused with comparison. We need to ask ourselves what are the core values of our sports program. When we strive to provide access to sports for our kids, what are our intentions? In a survey of youth sport coaches (Shields et al., 2005), 42 percent of the respondents indicated that they had loudly argued with the game official following a bad call. In addition, 36 percent reported that they angrily yelled at a player for making a mistake. Coaches, as educators, have a crucial role in the social and physical growth of our children. Our behaviors define the culture of the athletic community and have a great impact on how our athletes think, play, and act.

HALF-TIME: COMMON MYTHS IN COACHING

A common myth in coaching is that negative and demeaning comments and practices help prepare athletes for the real world on and off the playing field. We must accept responsibility for our actions and be certain that they are not hindering our mission and philosophy for sport programs. Participation in athletics has been crucial in providing a sense of belonging and reason for kids to try harder in school. They know they have to make good grades to play and try their best. Coaches make a difference every day in the lives of their student athletes. If bullying behaviors enter the playing field, how many kids would not play sports? How would not coming to practice and going out for a sport impact overall academic achievement and high school dropout rates?

Recall your best experience in sports. Most likely it involved empowering athletes to do extraordinary things. Building relationships with athletes and teaching them to value their teammates and work as a team provides great results in the culture as well as on the scoreboard.

Student athletes lose their confidence and self-image from constant put-downs and disparaging comments about ability, gender. or behavior. Piek and colleagues (2005) found a direct correlation between bullying and self-worth, particularly in youth who have coordination issues. This is important to coaches because students who have even a minor issue may suffer greatly from bullying. Coaches need to focus on not only the bullying behavior but the impact of the behavior on the athletes in their charge. When athletes are bullied for any reason it can be devastating and impact their confidence and attitude toward the sport.

Coaches can be demanding without being demeaning. Strict, tough, and demanding are descriptors of a great coach. Dehumanizing, rude, and sarcastic are not. For many of our adolescent athletes, perception is reality. Their self-image is defined in how they are regarded by others. Sports participation often helps improve self-image. However, when these athletes are on the receiving end of ridicule and bullying behaviors there may be cause for concern that leads to severe and long-term consequences.

We have seen in sports poor behaviors of parents, coaches, athletes, and spectators. We often see this viewed as funny or just acts in the heat of the moment. Can we say that we want good sportsmanship and allow such behaviors? Coaches have the power to set the tone in regard to expected behaviors and what is absolutely unacceptable and stay the course.

Research shows that students who have a positive connection to their schools and have nonaggressive relationships with their peers tend to be more successful both in athletics and in school. It makes sense to be certain that the climate in the locker room is one of respect because these attitudes not only affect what is happening at that time but also carry into every aspect of the athletes' life. Coaches play a big part in reinforcing positive behavior and encouraging acceptance and ultimately good sportsmanship and team cohesion.

POSTGAME: PROMOTING SPORTSMANSHIP

Promoting good sportsmanship has many aspects, but it is safe to say that it begins with the ethical behavior of the coach. Most states have high school athletic associations that develop standards and provide guidance for coaches. The primary theme of these ethical guidelines is that the coach is primarily a teacher. For the athlete, the locker room and the playing field or pool is a classroom where life lessons are learned. Athletes are there because they choose to participate, and since that participation is hands-on, they are more likely to remember what they learn.

Coaches need to be aware that they are above all role models for their athletes. Every word and action has the potential to have a profound impact on their athletes. Most athletic associations view coaches as teachers first. But that teaching goes well beyond the instruction of the sport. It is about so much more than how to pass a ball, shoot a puck, or lengthen a stroke. It is about modeling behavior that matches the expectations of good sportsmanlike behavior.

When coaches behave inappropriately and the behavior goes unaddressed, we are sending the message that it is okay. If we are to break the existing culture that any type of bullying behavior makes you strong and tough, it has to begin with the coach. Our goal and mission is to help kids feel accepted rather than rejected. They need to feel the coach is on their side while pushing them to reach new limits. We need to get to the point that the behaviors in the locker room are the same regardless of whether the coach is watching or not. This begins with modeling behavior that reflects the highest moral character.

Coaches need to build a team, yet at the same time they need to recognize and develop the self-image of each member of the team. While that may sound confusing, a team that works together needs to have members that are capable, self-reliant, and confident enough to support the success of one for the benefit of all. In other words, the athlete needs to understand that being the one who passes the ball is as important as the one who scores.

The development of self-worth is crucial to the athletes, who are young people still growing and developing—not just physically but socially and emotionally as well. Therefore it is important that the coach choose ways to communicate with athletes that are respectful as well as instructional.

How many times have we heard a coach say something like "You look like a bunch of girls out there" to a group of boys? Even though that is relatively benign in comparison to some things that can and have been said in the confines of the locker room, comments such as this can be devastating. Again, the focus needs to be on modeling the behavior we expect from athletes. If a coach is addressing the athletes in a disrespectful manner, in turn the athletes will treat one another similarly and the lessons of good sportsmanship will be lost.

The coach is the primary representative of the school in the athletic arena. That means that the decorum of the coach represents the value system and goals of the school. It is very important that the coach puts a best foot forward as an ambassador to a winning team; it sends a powerful message to everyone about good sportsmanship.

Athletics are extracurricular activities and are an excellent arena to teach students life skills in the area of time management and goal setting such as these:

- Getting to practice on time
- Being prepared with all the necessary equipment
- Working to the best of their ability
- Setting personal goals
- Supporting other team members

These skills can be an integral part of the influence of a coach.

Good sportsmanship essentially is a part of character education. In other words, the work of the coach is to teach these skills along with teamwork, personal discipline, and the fundamentals of the sport. These skills can have long-term positive impact on athletes. Berkowitz and Bier (2007) support the notion that character education targets a particular portion of psychological characteristics that enable and motivate young people to be socially responsible, ethical, and independent. Coaches play an integral role in developing fundamental prosocial choices and moral values in our athletes. Good sportsmanship is about giving athletes the moral compass by which they can make the right choices as they navigate through their lives. There are many teachable moments in the locker room and on the field. Coaches need to look at this as an opportunity to teach these principles in the physical setting.

OVERTIME: PROMOTING SPORTSMANSHIP—THE PHYSICAL SIDE

The coach is also responsible for providing a safe environment for both practice and competition. This goes far beyond the physical setting. It includes the culture and social environment. It is difficult for some to go beyond the notion of what type of behavior may be acceptable under the domain of sports that would not be acceptable in any other setting.

The coach in the story highlighted in this chapter felt that the towel snapping was okay. If that happened in another setting it would be immediately obvious that it was unacceptable. So it is very important that an attitude of respect begins with the coach. Modeling behavior is not something that should have specific areas—it should be an integral part of the core character of a leader. However, some areas where the coach can model respect include:

- Dealing with assistant coaches and volunteers in the athletic program and having the same standards
- Responding to complaints of bullying
- Promoting and demonstrating a set of training expectations and rules
- Abstaining from alcohol and tobacco
- Linking academic success to athletic success
- Above all—being modest in victory and gracious in defeat

Leadership is a term that is very closely related to athletics, as athletes are often regarded as leaders within the school community. This translates into influencing these students to remember that they need to demonstrate qualities that are in turn models for the entire school. It sets a climate that goes back to the expectations and example set by the coach.

Many coaches talk about the importance of communication with their athletes. This is a key to conveying the values the coach feels crucial to building not only a team but also future leaders. There needs to be a plan for developing and continuing the lines of communication. This can be as simple as doing these things:

- Clearly post office hours.
- Distribute a handbook with rules and expectations.
- Meet regularly with staff.
- Hold formal meetings with the athletes.
- Frequent conversations with each individual on the team.
- Focus on the strengths of each student and always end on a positive note when there needs to be instruction for skills improvement.

For the coach, the need for communication goes well beyond the locker room. The coach needs to reach out to the community about the values and goals of the athletic program. When the team either wins or loses, the local media will look to the coach for comments. To set the tone for the climate, the coach must always be positive and supportive of the team. Saying that the other team played a great game is much better than making excuses or accusations of unfairness. Gracious and dignified acceptance of a loss or modest and generous acknowledgment of a win can be a powerful lesson. It was Vince Lombardi that said, "If you cannot accept losing, you cannot accept winning."

In like manner it is important that the coach regard the decisions of the game official with the greatest respect. Not all decisions will be correct or fair, but the most important thing is that good sportsmanship means to accept them as part of the game. Certainly the coach is well within the parameters of expectation to protest a game call—but that can be done in a respectful way. We have all seen a coach kick dirt or spit on a game official—that is the worst example of how a role model should respond. One cannot expect students to respect their peers if the coach does not reflect that same behavior.

It is also important for the coach to communicate with parents of the athletes and partner up with them. This could be the road to develop the physical abilities of athletes and, more important, build character. Parents should have a copy of the handbook, which has the rules for the sport and the expectations of the coach.

Parents feel comfortable when the coach knows their child and his abilities. Communicating with parents is central to developing trust and collaboration focused on success—for the team and the development of the student.

By knowing each member of the team the coach can work with each individual personality to foster good judgment and initiative. These skills combined together help to create a climate where students become a cohesive unit that will work and get along together to attain success as a team.

Regardless of the sport, there is always a measure of physical risk. In contact sports, adherence to rules is vitally important. Injury prevention is something that must be an integral part of the athletic program. When an injury occurs the coach needs to have a process of handling the injury and then communication with the family and other key interested parties. This preparation and caring contribute to the building of a positive climate and a feeling of security. Pepler (2006) stated that in order to eliminate bullying behavior, focus needs to be on a social architecture that requires that adults focus on the social dynamics of children's groups and create a social context that promotes positive peer interactions and dissipates contexts that foster negative interactions.

The world of athletics is about performance at the peak of physical capabilities. While this is a very personal, individual thing, it is crucial that the coach model personal fitness and healthy nutrition. When dealing with youth sports this is crucial because these youngsters are looking to their coach at an age when they will emulate the examples of those whom they admire. The teaching of good nutrition should also be a part of their athletic program.

This is a message that can be part of a lifelong practice. While winning is very important, coaching at the youth level is also about teaching. A healthy lifestyle that is part of the athletic program is about respect for one's own body and that is a fundamental lesson for all young athletes. Respect for others begins with respecting oneself and that notion is central to bullying prevention.

Bullying is much more than what is occurring between the one who is actively bullying and the one being victimized. Everyone is impacted and this includes the bystanders.

The average instance of bullying is brief—less than a minute. In addition the observational research of Craig, Pepler, and Atlas (2000) has shown that teachers intervened in only one of twenty-five instances of bullying. It is impossible for adults alone to witness and respond to every instance; therefore it takes everyone to solve this problem. Bystanders by their very presence when bullying occurs make a choice—to participate, to intervene, or to ignore the situation. To eliminate the difficulty we need to understand the role of bystanders and how we can empower them to know the best ways to intervene.

Figure 4.1 describes the varied types of roles students can play in a bullying incident. It is important to recognize these roles to fully understand that bullying is much more than what happens between the student who bullies and the onlookers who have the power to accelerate or stop this destructive behavior. We identify them according to their behavior as bullying aggressor, bully enforcer, and bully supporter.

Bullying Supporter
- Present when the bullying occurs
- Supports the behavior by approval
- Would not initiate the behavior independently

Bullying Enforcer
- Encourages the behavior
- May participate in the bullying behavior
- Capable of initiating bullying behavior

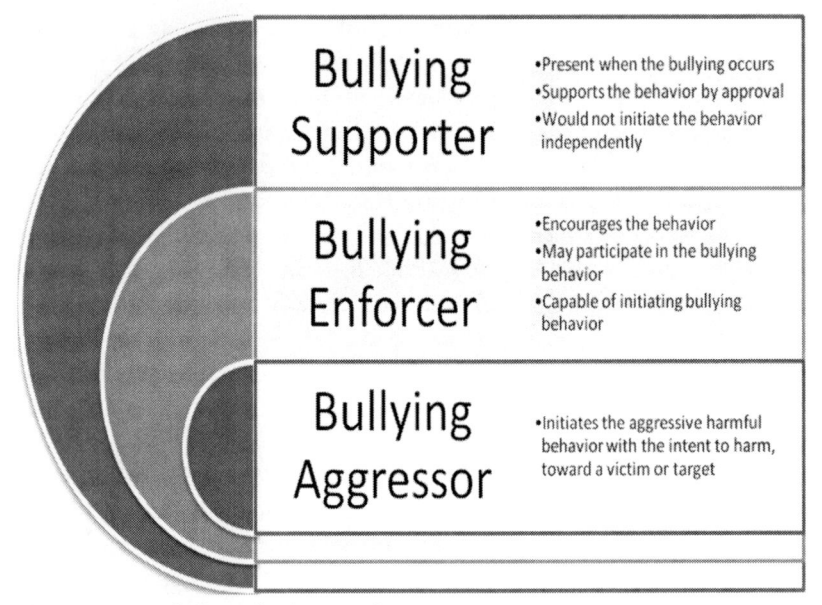

Bullying Aggressor
- Initiates the aggressive harmful behavior with the intent to harm, toward a victim or target

Figure 4.1. Bullying Behavior Graph

Bullying behavior is often initiated by one aggressor, termed the *bullying aggressor*. This behavior usually happens in a group in front of others. In addition to the aggressor, other athletes that are present participate in different ways. They become part of the situation whether or not they engage in bullying behaviors. Peer approval is given to the bullying aggressor by the dynamics of the bully enforcer and bully supporter. This dynamic left unchecked is a recipe for disaster.

Bully enforcers play a role in contributing to the bullying incident. They seek opportunities to both engage in bullying behaviors and encourage others to join in. Attention must be directed to bully enforcers to provide consequences as they may be future perpetrators and own a part of the responsibility for the victimization.

The bully supporter encourages the action and in some instances will participate in a peripheral way via cheering, taunting, or taking a turn at the victimization. This is of concern to the athletic culture because bullying behaviors are seen as both acceptable and even amusing. In most instances, they will not initiate the behavior but they are the ones that always seem to be right in the middle of things. When questioned, their response is often, "I didn't do anything." It must be made clear that their presence escalates the bullying and is a source of humiliation for the victim. When all athletes understand how they contribute to the culture of bullying, we can minimize and even reduce these behaviors. We want to send the message that this is a community, a team, and we protect and respect one another.

We are not promoting stereotypes for those who use bullying behavior but rather helping clarify the levels of involvement that students can have in a bullying incident. These categories help to illustrate the fact that students who are present contribute in a peripheral way to the bullying. In addition, these students need to understand their social responsibility to their peers and consequences associated with any level of participation.

Our athletes witness many of the bullying behaviors that threaten the athletic experience. Research supports that helping bystanders understand their role is a great tool for preventing bullying. In regard to bystanders, there are some distinct profiles (figure 4.2). By understanding these

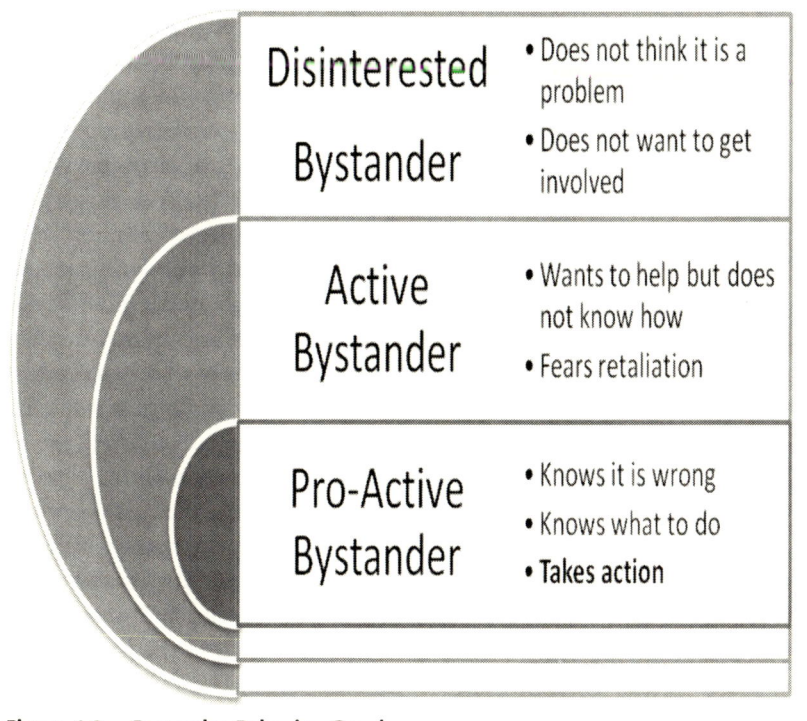

Disinterested Bystander	• Does not think it is a problem • Does not want to get involved
Active Bystander	• Wants to help but does not know how • Fears retaliation
Pro-Active Bystander	• Knows it is wrong • Knows what to do • **Takes action**

Figure 4.2.   Bystander Behavior Graph

- I will do my best to organize practices that are fun and challenging for all my players.
- I will lead by example in demonstrating fair play and sportsmanship to all my players.
- I will provide a sports environment for my team that is free of drugs, tobacco, and alcohol, and I will refrain from their use at all youth sports events.
- I will be knowledgeable in the rules of each sport that I coach, and I will teach these rules to my players.
- I will use those coaching techniques appropriate for all of the skills that I teach.
- I will remember that I am a youth sports coach, and that the game is for children and not adults.

tioned, their response is often, "I didn't do anything." It must be made clear that their presence escalates the bullying and is a source of humiliation for the victim. When all athletes understand how they contribute to the culture of bullying, we can minimize and even reduce these behaviors. We want to send the message that this is a community, a team, and we protect and respect one another.

We are not promoting stereotypes for those who use bullying behavior but rather helping clarify the levels of involvement that students can have in a bullying incident. These categories help to illustrate the fact that students who are present contribute in a peripheral way to the bullying. In addition, these students need to understand their social responsibility to their peers and consequences associated with any level of participation.

Our athletes witness many of the bullying behaviors that threaten the athletic experience. Research supports that helping bystanders understand their role is a great tool for preventing bullying. In regard to bystanders, there are some distinct profiles (figure 4.2). By understanding these

Disinterested Bystander	• Does not think it is a problem • Does not want to get involved
Active Bystander	• Wants to help but does not know how • Fears retaliation
Pro-Active Bystander	• Knows it is wrong • Knows what to do • **Takes action**

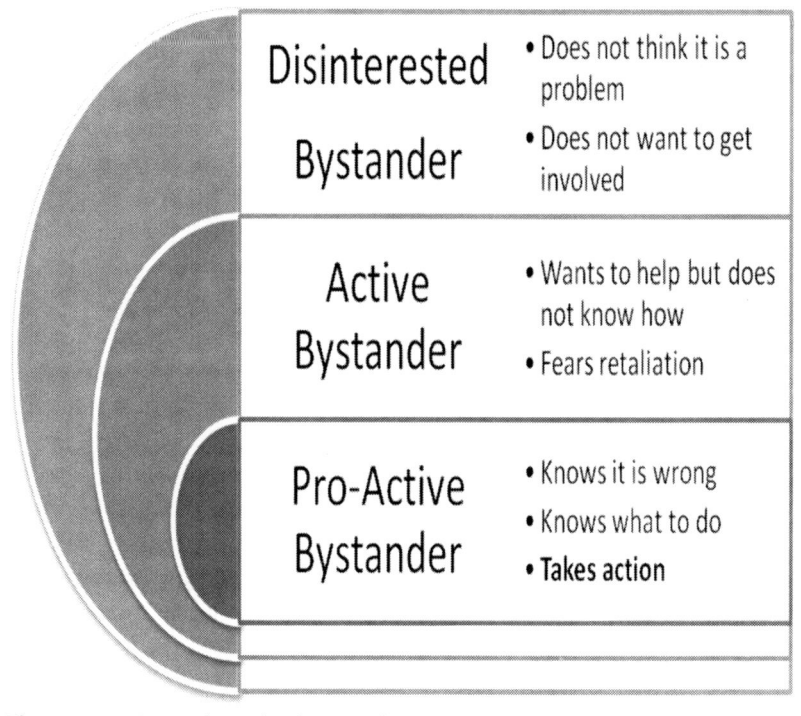

Figure 4.2. Bystander Behavior Graph

profiles, it is easier to consider what needs to be done to encourage all bystanders to respond appropriately when someone is being victimized. When bystanders are proactive to stop the behavior and that becomes the norm, bullying dramatically decreases.

Disinterested bystanders do not think bullying is a problem. They would say it happens to everyone. It may have even happened to them in the past. They may feel that there would be retaliation if they get involved. In any case these are bystanders that will not get involved—they do not condone the behavior, but they simply feel that is it not their business.

Active bystanders realize that bullying is not okay, that it is wrong and even hurtful. However, they usually sit by and take no actions to stop the bullying or assist the victim. They would help if they knew what to do and they did not have to fear retaliation from those who are bullying. Most kids fall into this group and already have the necessary level of empathy for the victim. With a little encouragement and assistance they may be guided to intervene in a way that is both comfortable and safe. These bystanders are pivotal to changing the culture. In other words, since they already understand that bullying is happening and it is wrong, all they need is information about the best way to help.

The goal is to encourage all athletes—all students for that matter—to respond as proactive bystanders. This is the point of character that is behind good sportsmanship. These athletes are the leaders who step in and stop the behaviors or help the victim. They will recognize bullying behavior and make a decision about how best to help with little concern about retaliation or losing their friends or status on the team. They know bullying is wrong; they know what to do and most importantly they take action. We need to talk to all athletes about how to respond when they see bullying, shifting them with support and encouragement. Certainly there are instances where students will change from one type of bystander to the other, depending on who or what is involved. The intention of the levels of bystanders serve to help create the best of sportsmanship in moving athletes to proactive behavior that prevents bullying and serves as a role model. Earlier we discussed the ability for athletes to serve as leaders for each other and the general school population. They may lead on and off the field by exemplary bystander behaviors learned and modeled by the coaches, parents, and peers.

Regardless, we need to both promote and praise the courage of the bystander. There are many ways that athletes are rewarded for their achievements, so in most cases this is just about adding another category. For example, a simple "Good boy" or "Way to go" for doing the right thing would send a powerful message that good sportsmanship and character is important to coaches and the sport.

We have asked many athletes to tell us about their experience with bullying and they still see some bullying behavior as normal behaviors that are a regular part of their athletic lives. This illustrates the need to educate athletes, especially bystanders, to recognize bullying and to respond appropriately. You can use figures 4.1 and 4.2 as an illustration of the roles young athletes can take in a bullying incident. By understanding these roles, you can decide how best to handle those that are present when bullying occurs and whether or not there are consequences for the bullying behavior. There needs to be a discussion about what could have been done to stop the behavior.

We need to expand our view of bullying to include the bystander and the best ways to reduce the behavior and empower courage to act. Research shows that more than half the time when there is bystander intervention the bullying stops within 10 seconds (Pepler & Craig, 1997). The responsibility to respond to help the victim needs to be taught as part of the character education expectations of athletes in demonstrating good sportsmanship. This will help with the vision that every member of the team is a proactive bystander. The best way to model that vision is by modeling the Coaches' Code of Ethics at each and every practice and game. Below is an example of a Coaches' Pledge based on the Code of Ethics by the National Alliance for Youth Sports.

- I hereby pledge to live up to my certification as a NYSCA coach by following the NYSCA Coaches' Code of Ethics.
- I will place the emotional and physical well-being of my players ahead of any personal desire to win.
- I will treat each player as an individual, remembering the large range of emotional and physical development for the same age group.
- I will do my best to provide a safe playing situation for my players.
- I promise to review and practice basic first aid principles needed to treat injuries of my players.

- I will do my best to organize practices that are fun and challenging for all my players.
- I will lead by example in demonstrating fair play and sportsmanship to all my players.
- I will provide a sports environment for my team that is free of drugs, tobacco, and alcohol, and I will refrain from their use at all youth sports events.
- I will be knowledgeable in the rules of each sport that I coach, and I will teach these rules to my players.
- I will use those coaching techniques appropriate for all of the skills that I teach.
- I will remember that I am a youth sports coach, and that the game is for children and not adults.

5

FANS: THE VIEW FROM THE GRANDSTANDS

STORIES FROM THE SIDELINES

In January 2008 the student fans of a suburban high school hockey team were not allowed to attend a hockey game because of rowdiness at the previous hockey game. The fans chanted obscenities and were insulting and disruptive during the game. The officials from the Statewide Interscholastic Association were in attendance to monitor the behavior of the fans because of an unruly history. During the game these officials also became objects of taunts and heckling from members of the crowd.

When questioned about the incident the hockey coach took a defensive position on the behavior of the fans and seemed to sweep it under the carpet. He said that while he felt that generally speaking the fans were great they had occasionally crossed the line. During an interview with the press, he said that he did not understand why the fans weren't able to attend the game but would yield to the decision of the school officials and not allow the fans to attend the game. This was not the first time that fans were unruly and disruptive and it seemed to be widespread, particularly when there were no consequences for unacceptable fan behavior.

Unfortunately this type of fan behavior has become far too commonplace. For all the talk about good sportsmanship, there still remains a standard of unacceptable fan behavior. Rowdiness and rude disruptive behavior are symptoms of a culture that has been supported and encouraged. We should be aware of the contagious nature of crowd behavior and that it is fueled by a sense that it is okay in this setting. Our kids recognize this behavior. A 2001 survey by *Sports Illustrated for Kids* revealed that 74 percent said they had witnessed out-of-control adults at their games, and the two most commonly observed types of bad behavior were parents yelling at children and parents yelling at officials or coaches.

The National Association of Sports Officials has been recording some of the more serious incidents of fan violence since 1996 and they seem to be occurring with more frequency all over America and in a myriad of sports. In Hampton, Pennsylvania, a parent body-slammed a high school referee after the official ordered the man's wife out of the gym for allegedly yelling obscenities during a basketball game. The referee was treated for a concussion after the February 2004 attack. The parent was charged with disorderly conduct and assault and fined $300.

In New Jersey, a referee was slugged in the head and neck after ejecting a Clayton High School player with minutes left in a 2004 scoreless game. The player, who had received a yellow card earlier in the game for incidental cursing, was given a red card for taunting. The player was charged with aggravated assault and released in the custody of his parents.

At a fifth grade Little League basketball game in Adair County, Kentucky, one of the fathers physically confronted the game official during halftime after the official ejected several players for a fight that broke out during the first half of the game. In Illinois a parent was charged with two counts of aggravated battery and one count of battery after allegedly charging onto the field and attempting to choke the game official during a 2003 high school football game. The athletic director prosecuted to the full extent of the law.

A father of a Kentucky T-ball youth baseball player was briefly jailed after an outburst against an umpire during a game involving five- and six-year-olds. The parent was accused of threatening to beat the umpire moments before walking onto the field and starting a fight. A girl who was playing in the game suffered a minor injury when she was struck in the face during the scuffle. This 2003 incident resulted in the parent receiving a five-year ban from attending sport events in Davis County. These are just a few of the many fans whose behavior is damaging to the athletic arena and jeopardizes the mental and physical health of our young athletes.

A major player for addressing this behavior lies with the coach. This is about setting a tone of respect and a system of values that is reflected in the way the coach interacts with every single person associated with the athletic program and beyond. This applies to fans as well. A model for behavior leadership and good sportsmanship begins with the coach and must be addressed by the coach, enforced by the coach, and most importantly supported by the director of athletics.

KICKOFF

You do not have to look far to see an example of unacceptable fan behavior. We see it at all levels from the Little League to the big leagues—adults who use bullying behavior under the guise of being loyal fans. Cursing and other choice names are used by fans from opposing teams. A little booing may seem harmless, but unchecked these types of behaviors may and do escalate to bullying and threatening behavior. This type of behavior is often captured by the media and our kids are exposed to it. It becomes material for jokes and may be unintentionally reinforced as funny behavior.

Violence breeds violence and bullying behaviors breed other bullying behaviors. Thus we must reinforce that these behaviors are unacceptable under any circumstances. The athletic field must be welcoming to all the children and their interests, strengths, and weaknesses. If children are welcomed and recognized with importance and their potential, amazing results will occur. When spectators respond with rude and disparaging comments during the game, the athletes suffer. The behaviors of these spectators, when left unchecked, set the tone of negativity and provide a culture that counteracts the benefits of sports.

Children hold on to the attitudes that adults express and carry them around far too long. Research by Watson (2006) found that there were positive long-term effects of character education. This validates the need to enforce behavior we wish to see from youth in the future. We must speak and act in a language they understand, and appreciate and convey a message we want them to internalize. Too often children don't take sarcasm and put-downs as just fan talk—instead it becomes personal.

Shock, horror, and disgust would be easy to generate at many of the words emanating from fans in the stands. We must ask ourselves what it is about our culture that evokes and permits such responses. Why is this permitted and even condoned? Making light of these behaviors is wrong, unacceptable, and definitely fixable.

In sports, although most of the experiences for young people are excellent, too many others fall into an unhealthy emotional state because of hurtful experiences. These experiences can and often do tear down their self-esteem. Participation in sports can be an essential component of developing self-assured healthy kids. However, in a few seconds those fans watching can and sometimes do cause and provoke adverse reactions that counteract all the factors in athletics that inspire greatness. This happens with mean and degrading jeers and insults hurled at the players from the stands.

Fans must be reminded to use language and body gestures that foster respect. They should use their cheers and words to build confidence that helps these athletes work harder and strive for excellence. Left unchecked, tempers and belittling words can be very threatening and cause anxiety. These leave athletes feeling unworthy and that they are treated "as less," which will automatically effect their performance.

As groups of fans we should use words and expressions that are not demeaning. For example, we must teach appropriateness, recognize ethical considerations, and act as soon as a perpetrator opens his mouth. These remarks can become defining moments for kids. The way we display ourselves and speak in the stands determines the culture of how we play the game, and being demanding without being demeaning is the only route to take. The good news is that we can take positive steps to reverse this destructive trend of behavior.

HALFTIME:
PARENT RESPONSIBILITIES

Following certain negative patterns of behaviors from fans, athletes accept and get used to the yelling, screaming, and belittling that accompany certain games and practices. For some young children these behaviors are the fine line between motivating and emotional abuse. Every now and then we need to give kids a pep talk to get them to go the extra mile or practice and pay attention a little bit more. However, it is crucial that we understand the knockdown of an athlete's spirit, which definitely hinders achieving success and ability to do well and enjoy the sport.

All in all, what we want is to promote self-esteem and a healthy lifestyle through participation in sports. We certainly don't want to contribute to or cause anxiety, depression, or a poor self-image. We want to move all athletes toward their best performance. We may create some superstars who go on to play professionally, but in reality, most of the athletes we touch we hope will continue a love for the sport and the exercise habits, teamwork skills, and discipline gained from their involvement over the years.

As parents, we must examine our behaviors and how we express ourselves and how it all impacts our child. We certainly get upset when our children do things in public that embarrass us. Well, this is a two-way street and children have been subjected to comments from parents. Every time a certain child struggles a little with his or her game, a parent may shout out to the next player to get ready because this one is going to strike out or wonder aloud why they let him play on this team.

It is unimaginable to allow kids who struggle with reading or math to be subjected to this kind of ridicule. It is difficult to understand why many fans don't have the boundaries to respect all members of a team and keep disrespectful comments to themselves. When bystander parents allow these comments by keeping quiet or minding their own business, we are dismissing bullying behavior. Silence constitutes an agreement that the behavior is okay.

On other occasions, we have seen parents who have exhibited bullying behaviors toward a coach or referee. It is very important to note that every altercation that involves a disagreement between a coach or parent is bullying. Sometimes conflicts develop among adults but there is a time and place for all of these types of behaviors. Every coach, referee, and parent will experience a time when they will have to deal with a complaint; however, resolving it should be done in the proper manner with respect. When there is a problem with a parent the eight tips in figure 5.1 are crucial for the coach to effectively deal with these complaints. Now let's look at the points in figure 5.1 in more detail.

1. Don't discuss the conflict at the game in front of the athletes. The message to the athletes must be that the coach is in charge so it is important to respectfully refuse to discuss issues in front of the athletes. Also it is crucial that the conflicts be diffused by taking time to cool off before the discussion. Often this allows the people involved an opportunity to think

56   *Chapter 5*

1. Don't discuss the conflict at the game in front of the athletes.

2. Don't dismiss the problem but agree to set a convenient time to hear the complaint.

3. Be an active listener without interrupting or becoming defensive or visibly upset by the complaint or issue.

4. Show empathy and ask enough questions to clarify the issue in question.

5. Demonstrate that you are concerned and are willing to work together to solve the issue.

6. Don't make promises you cannot keep but thank them for sharing their concern and advise them to please contact you if there is ever anything else they want to discuss.

7. Create a comfortable atmosphere where all comments and ideas are welcome.

8. Follow up by inquiring on the situation or reporting some positive behaviors or outcomes when applicable.

Figure 5.1. Eight Tips for Coaches when dealing with partent complaints.

and get the facts before the meeting with the coach. In general this leads to a more calm and rational meeting. It also gives both parties the chance to discuss the issue in private.

2. Don't dismiss the problem but agree to set a convenient time to hear the complaint. When an issue comes up, it is important to acknowledge that you are willing to discuss it at the proper time and place. Before the discussion is over, set an appointment for the interview. This sends a very important message that you are listening. It by no means is an agreement that anything will change; rather it means that you are willing to take time to listen. This shows respect and that can go a long way when the issue is controversial.

3. Be an active listener without interrupting or becoming defensive or visibly upset by the complaint or issue. Active listening is a way of listening and responding to another person that improves mutual understanding. It involves listening to what the other person is saying and repeating for clarification. When there is a conflict, listening closely to the other person helps to clarify not only the facts but the feelings behind them. When a coach is talking to a parent, it is important to realize that above all they are talking about their child. There can be strong emotion and first and foremost a parent is looking to be heard.

Active listening has several benefits. First, it forces people to listen closely to others. Second, it avoids misunderstandings, as people have to confirm that they do really understand what another person has said. Third, it tends to open people up, to get them to say more. When people are in conflict, they often contradict each other, denying the opponent the opportunity to describe their own position. However, if they feel that you are really attuned to their concerns and want to listen, they are likely to explain in detail what they feel and why.

If both parties to a conflict do this, the chances of being able to develop a solution to their mutual problem becomes much greater. As a result everyone benefits, including the athletes. This does not mean that coaches have to give in to the wishes and directions of parents. It simply means that listening helps to build relationships.

4. Show empathy and ask enough questions to clarify the issue in question. By asking appropriate questions, you can get a clear picture of the issue. Showing empathy can be difficult, particularly when the other person is angry. But that empathy can serve as a powerful example for the athletes that look to the adults for examples of how to handle conflict.

5. Demonstrate that you are concerned and are willing to work together to solve the issue. This can be as simple as taking time to offer a variety of suggestions for a solution. Also when the solution is one that involves the parent, it gives parents and coaches an opportunity to work together toward a common goal. This can happen even in cases, for instance, where the parent is looking for something that is not feasible. He or she can become involved with the team in another capacity.

6. Don't make promises you cannot keep, but thank them for sharing their concern and advise them to please contact you if there is ever anything else they want to discuss.

7. Create a comfortable atmosphere where all comments and ideas are welcome. This is the center of a climate and culture that is respectful. It is about relationships where there is communication—not just when there are problems, but communication on a regular basis.

8. Follow up by inquiring on the situation or reporting some positive behaviors or outcomes when applicable. Outreach to see how things are going not only shows genuine caring but also keeps the door open for regular communication. This communication needs to fall under the definition of respectful and demanding, and it will set the tone for a winning team.

POSTGAME: DEMANDING VERSUS DEMEANING

The continuum between demeaning and demanding left unchecked may result in long-term risks and consequences.

Demeaning behaviors involve:

- Dirty looks
- Name-calling
- Cursing
- Humiliation
- Calling a boy a faggot, homo, queer, sissy, or girl
- Calling a girl a dike, butch, or lesbo
- Ethnic slurs
- Isolating a player from his team
- Yelling and screaming that causes public embarrassment

Demanding behaviors involve:

- Motivating athletes to try harder
- Encouraging efforts for each individual to go beyond the ordinary
- Changing behaviors while building confidence
- Promoting a healthy lifestyle
- Imposing fair, consistent consequences
- Proving that character is paramount
- Discouraging all instances of bad behavior

- Promoting team loyalty and commitment
- Promoting kindness, understanding, and patience

Obnoxious and disrespectful comments and behaviors that go unaddressed may lead to violence and place athletes, fans, and coaches in danger. There have been many instances of a fan losing control at a sporting event like the mom or dad that got in a physical fight in front of children at a Little League game. Nationally there have been some serious legal cases that have ended with prison time for those participants. After a fight between parents in a hockey rink in Reading, Massachusetts, one parent died. This horrific scene played out in front of parents and the young hockey players. In June 2000 the hockey dad was sentenced to prison for involuntary manslaughter.

In those instances it is more than those who are involved that are injured. The bystanders, including younger siblings and other athletes watching, may think the fighting is okay behavior and associate violence with athletics. Bullying behaviors are an escalating trajectory and fan behavior may intensify the nature of bullying (figure 5.2). Athletes look to their peers and the adults around them for what is acceptable and unacceptable behavior. Coaches have a responsibility to minimize fan behaviors that counteract the benefits of sports.

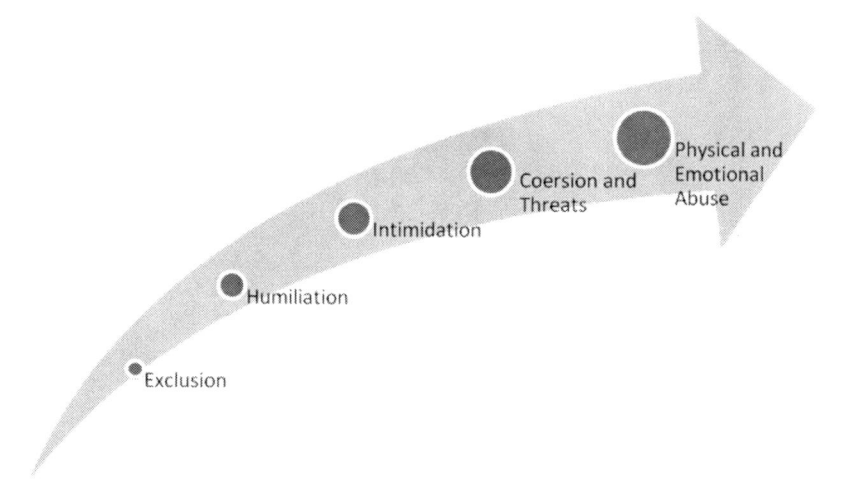

Figure 5.2. Bullying Behavior Escalating Trajectory

1. Obtain coaches and staff support as well as other parents for bullying prevention. Involve everyone!

2. Praise kindness and good sportsmanship!

3. Listen & respond appropriately to your athlete when there are reports of bullying.

4. Model respectful spectator behavior when at games/meets. Expect the same from other onlookers.

5. Support the coaches when they are dealing with bullying incidents.

Figure 5.3. Five Helpful Tips for Parents to Prevent Bullying in Athletics

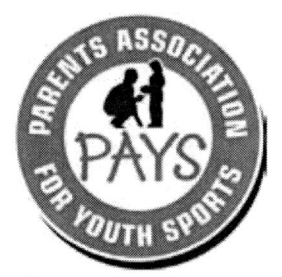

Figure 5.4. PAYS

There is no place for disrespectful conduct of any sort on the sidelines. Profanity, obscene gestures, offensive remarks of a sexual nature, or other actions demean individuals or teams. Coaches, referees, and other game officials must be treated respectfully. Any disagreements or conflicts should be handled professionally and respectfully. Reflecting on our words and actions to be certain that all behaviors are demanding without being demeaning are crucial to fans that support our athletes and the sport. Parents may want to reflect on some practical and helpful tips to help them help their athletes have a bully-free athletic environment (figures 5.3, 5.4).

Parents' Code of Ethics

I hereby pledge to provide positive support, care, and encouragement for my child participating in youth sports by following this PAYS Parents' Code of Ethics:

- I will encourage good sportsmanship by demonstrating positive support for all players, coaches, and officials at every game, practice, or other youth sports event.
- I will place the emotional and physical well-being of my child ahead of a personal desire to win.
- I will insist that my child play in a safe and healthy environment.
- I will require that my child's coach be trained in the responsibilities of being a youth sports coach and that the coach upholds the Coaches' Code of Ethics.
- I will support coaches and officials working with my child, in order to encourage a positive and enjoyable experience for all.

- I will demand a sports environment for my child that is free from drugs, tobacco, and alcohol, and will refrain from their use at all youth sports events.
- I will remember that the game is for youths—not for adults.
- I will do my very best to make youth sports fun for my child.
- I will help my child enjoy the youth sports experience by doing whatever I can, such as being a respectful fan, assisting with coaching, or providing transportation.
- I will ask my child to treat other players, coaches, fans, and officials with respect regardless of race, sex, creed, or ability.
- I will read the National Standards for Youth Sports and do what I can to help all youth sports organizations implement and enforce them.

_____   _____

Parent Signature   Date
© National Alliance for Youth Sports
2050 Vista Parkway
West Palm Beach, FL 33406
(800) 729-2057 / FAX (561) 684-2546 pays@nays.org

6

THE PLAYBOOK: BEST PRACTICES—PREVENTION

When we discuss bullying prevention we find that good sportsmanship and character education become central to the discussion. Sportsmanship is about conduct in general. It is about the pathway by which athletes compete, win, lose, and learn life's lessons. Sportsmanship is about the ideals and expectations that come from competition and rivalry. It is about the value of stretching limits and reaching one's personal goals. Sportsmanship is about teaching values and the values that are taught through participation in athletics.

Teamwork is an integral part of sportsmanship. The personal sacrifices of the athlete are all part of being a team. It is about the goal for excellence, code of conduct, character, and a sense of camaraderie that makes lifelong friends beginning with a team. That is what sportsmanship can be at its best. However, despite goals and intentions, unfortunately bullying is a part of athletics. When we talk about best practices in bullying prevention, we are addressing bullying especially in athletics.

Best practices in bullying prevention are based on the data developed by examining the approaches that work best. To begin, let's review: bullying is a repeated, intentional, hurtful action that always involves an imbalance of power.

Best practices are based on reducing the risk factors for bullying. They are about the identification and prevention that addresses bullying and the culture that supports this behavior. In adolescence, support and encouragement from adults is crucial in reducing the risk of bullying behavior. Close positive association with the school or with the athletic team is very important. These associations and connections are what help our kids gain the skills that help them manage their life demands, ambitions, and goals (Woolley & Bowen, 2007). It is through the respect of the adults that the climate becomes comfortable and safe for the students and youth. This also applies to athletics. The goals of athletics involve competition and achievement and can be aligned with bullying prevention efforts when presented appropriately.

There is concern that warmth and compassion and a positive climate can be detrimental to the competitive nature of sports. The truth is our student athletes today have few places to build a sense of belonging, self-worth, and basic life skills. Families are often fragmented for a number of reasons including divorce and serious economic pressure. Because of these and many other factors, athletics has become central to how children feel about themselves.

How young people learn to cope with their own life stress is closely related to what they experience and observe. William Pollack, a founding member and fellow of the Society for the Psychological Study of Men and Masculinity, says boys are desperate to reveal their true feelings while at the same time conflicted about their need to fit the image of what they believe is masculine. In a 2006 study on this issue, Jesse Klein notes, "The hallmarks of normalized masculinity—hyper-masculine identification, athletics, fighting, distance from homosexuality, dominant relationships with girls, socioeconomic status, and disdain for academics—do not include alternative ways to build cultural capital when young men do not fit into rigid traditional social structures."

There is an underlying unwritten rule that says "boys don't cry" and that theme when reinforced can have a lifelong effect by stifling feelings, which can then lead to anger. This is an example of a stereotype or belief that may be hurting our male athletes.

We certainly don't want to encourage deliberately pushing young people to cry; however, we do need to seek ways to allow our boys to express themselves. We can build toughness and emotional strength and provide safe and respectful outlets for expression. We can utilize these best practices to create an atmosphere that supports both the emotional and physical development of athletes.

There are eight steps in best practices that have been developed to address bullying at its root—in the athletic arena. These steps can be grouped into two basic categories, prevention and intervention. Prevention is a very important part of bullying prevention. When there is prevention, there is an opportunity to plan and prepare so that bullying does not occur. The steps described in the best practices plan address a comprehensive approach that is geared to changing the climate that supports bullying behavior.

Prevention:

1. Obtain coach and staff support as well as parent backing for bullying prevention. Involve everyone!
2. Coordinate and collaborate with the school's bullying prevention activities and provide training for coaching staff, parents, and athletes.
3. Establish and enforce specific rules related to bullying behavior that are in line with similar school policies.
4. Include bullying prevention as part of the discussions about sportsmanship.

Intervention:

5. Praise kindness and good sportsmanship.
6. Address bullying consistently and appropriately when it happens.
7. Increase adult supervision in hot spots for bullying. Pay particular attention to athletes who are less skilled as they are more likely to be bullied.
8. Monitor and continue these efforts in order to sustain the changes over time and to change the climate.

You have probably heard the saying that prevention is the best medicine. In regard to bullying behaviors, prevention efforts are certainly the best tactics in sports. Now let's examine these prevention steps in more detail, keeping in mind that while we are talking about athletics these same principles apply beyond the locker room and the athletic field.

BEST PRACTICE 1

Obtain coach and staff support as well as parent backing for bullying prevention. Communication needs to go all around—between the parents, coaches, and athletes (figure 6.1). It is a team effort to prevent bullying—it

Athletes

Communication ← → Good Sportsmanship ← → Character Development ← → Communication

Communication

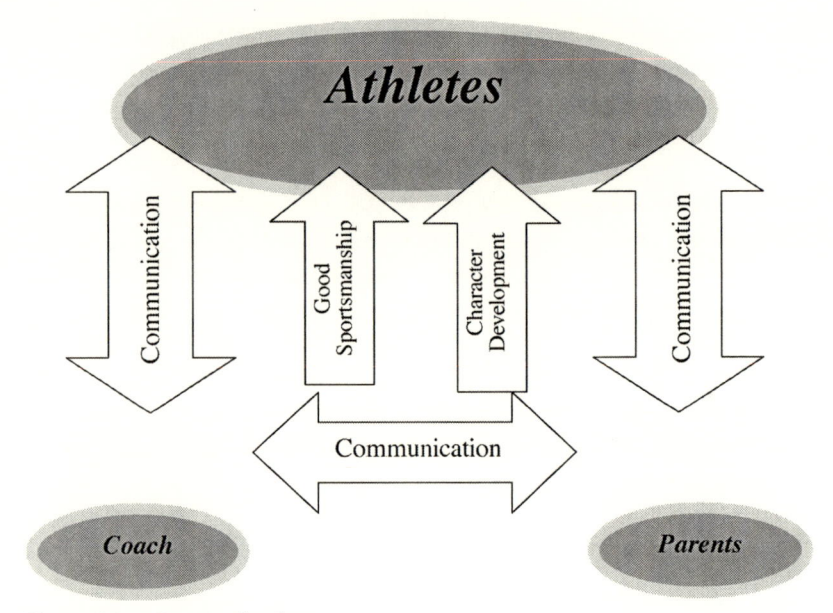

Coach **Parents**

Figure 6.1. Communication

takes influence from both the coach and the parents. Together their roles are crucial to teaching lifelong lessons about how people should be treated.

Coaches believe in good sportsmanship. This includes virtues such as fairness, self-control, courage, and persistence (Shields et al., 2005). Good sportsmanship is associated with interpersonal concepts of treating others and being treated fairly, maintaining self-control in dealing with others, and respect for both authority and opponents.

Bullying prevention when connected with good sportsmanship in this sense not only is compatible but also helps all team members. This belief needs to be extended to all the staff that is involved with the athletic program. By setting the example, coaches set the tone for the entire staff. Bullying prevention begins with them and needs to go beyond the example. The coach needs to expect accountability for how members of the team treat one another and when necessary involve the parent.

We know that parents are a valuable resource in the work of bullying prevention. Initially they need information regarding rules and expectations and this can be done by adding a section in the school handbook or through material of the league itself.

Traditionally there is a parent meeting before each season. During that meeting, the policy and plan for bullying prevention can be outlined for the parents. Often it is parents who ride on buses with athletes headed for an away game. In some instances coaches rely on parents to supervise practice drills. There are many other ways parents can be an invaluable part of any athletic program and it is important that they are involved in the process.

Parents must be notified in all instances that involve bullying behavior, whether the child is perpetrator or victim. This needs to be clearly stated in bullying prevention policies. When there has been parental involvement, it is easier on both parties to focus on dealing with the incident with the intent of addressing the bullying behavior. In other words, when parents are involved, the athlete is less defensive and more inclined to work toward a solution that works for everyone.

BEST PRACTICE 2

Coordinate and collaborate with the school's bullying prevention policy, activities, and training to include coaching staff, parents, and athletes. Policies need to include addressing bullying behavior at athletic events and school-sponsored events as well as transportation to and from those events.

Successful bullying prevention takes a community-wide initiative and a commitment from all the adults involved. Consistency is the key, so it makes sense to look to the school for policies and practices on bullying prevention. When the school is committed to a bullying prevention strategy, those values and strategies must include the athletic arena. When the school does not have a bullying prevention program, it presents a great opportunity for the athletic department to take the leadership role by influencing the school to adopt a plan. When an athletic program is not associated with a school, bullying prevention still can be coordinated with the staff, volunteers, parents, and athletes.

It is important to create a school and athletic atmosphere characterized by warmth, positive interest, and involvement with adults. This may seem contradictory to a competitive sport but in fact it is proven that a caring environment builds the basics of teamwork and success. It is the interpersonal connection of groups of athletes that makes a team.

The common goal of excellence through discipline and appropriate authority can lead to a cohesive team and winning.

By the nature of the athletic setting, coaches are the involved adults. It is how they approach their relationship with the athletes and how they discipline them that develops a caring and comfortable environment. When this environment is disrupted the consequences for unacceptable behavior should be addressed and ended.

More than anything it is the attitude behind setting the expectations and goals for the athletes that has a profound impact on the climate of the locker room. The coach can set clear goals for the team and hold the athletes to those standards at all times and in all arenas.

BEST PRACTICE 3

Establish and enforce rules in line with school policies related to bullying behavior. Defining clear rules is a crucial factor in dealing with bullying proactively. The athletic department or team league needs to have a written policy that is comprehensive and includes definitive procedures for dealing with bullying behaviors, developmental differences, and the athletic ability of each member of the team. This policy needs to encompass all forms of bullying including direct, indirect, and psychological forms, such as social exclusion and isolation, which are often omitted from behavior policies. In a time where most states have bullying prevention laws, there is much support for schools to address this issue. However, the lack of a general policy in the school should not preclude the coach from working with other coaches to develop a plan that works with the athletic teams.

Discipline begins with setting firm limits against unacceptable behavior. These need to be established by working with the staff, parents, and all stakeholders in the athletic program. Once there is a policy in place, simple no-bullying rules can be developed and posted in areas that are readily visible to the entire after-school community. The three rules recommended by Dan Olweus (1994) in his bullying prevention approach can be readily integrated into the athletic setting. These include:

1. We shall not bully other students.
2. We shall try to help students who are bullied.

3. We shall make a point to include students who are easily left out.

These rules are simple and straightforward yet they give the athlete clear direction about what is expected as well as what is unacceptable. These rules address both direct and indirect bullying and are specific about reporting the bullying behavior. Once the rules have been developed, there needs to be clear consequences or sanctions if they are broken.

Once there is a policy and rules, it is important to discuss them with the staff and athletes so everyone has a common understanding of bullying and how to handle it. Coaches and staff will need to discuss a plan for supervision and procedures for individuals that cause and carry out bullying. When determining sanctions for bullying behavior, everyone must consider the depth of the bullying and decide on the consequences.

The consequences for breaking the rules must be nonphysical and nonhostile and must be applied immediately upon recognition and considering the impact on the victim. It is important that all the adults act with authority. Kids respect adults they cannot manipulate, who act with authority and say, "You have broken the rules and this is not how we treat each other on this team, and therefore your consequence is. . . ."

By responding in this manner, you are being emphatic and supporting the values of good sportsmanship and meaning what you preach. This is not to be confused with an autocratic, insulting, and punitive response such as, "You idiot—do that again and you will take laps." Coaches are teachers and the playing field is a classroom. Threats do not work; actions do and are remembered. A basic test to see if a response is appropriate is to ask if it would be acceptable in the classroom. If it is something that would never be said in a classroom, then it does not belong in the athletic climate either.

While the focus is often solely on the negative consequences, it is important to remember that positive rewards reinforce prosocial behaviors by recognizing the athlete for doing the right thing. Athletic programs are always responding to success by awarding trophies, plaques, or other forms of recognition. In fact, good sportsmanship should be also recognized in this manner.

Therefore it is well within common practice to add an award for being a leader in bullying prevention. This could be for something positive, such as being a buddy or getting caught doing the right thing. However it is done, the important thing is that by publicly recognizing proper sportsmanship, you demonstrate support and reinforce positive behavior at the same time.

BEST PRACTICE 4

Integrate bullying prevention as part of the discussions about sportsmanship. The concepts and values that are integral to bullying prevention are a close match to the driving principles of good sportsmanship. Discipline, honesty, and integrity are components of every good sportsmanship program.

For the purpose of this discussion, when we talk about discipline, we mean that at regular practices and drills we integrate part of the discipline preparation and training for competition. This discipline provides a predictable structure that helps athletes to understand the connection between work and success. In other words, when a youth is part of a team that has regular training workouts, the discipline to attend those sessions and fully participate is part of why they feel confident in their ability and proud to be part of the team.

The idea of honesty is supported when athletes are encouraged to work to the best of their abilities, in other words work hard and give it their all. By putting the best effort possible into the practices, kids are learning a great life lesson of trying hard and persevering to reach their personal best.

This can also be demonstrated by the commitment of the coaches. They can reinforce the idea of honesty by working with the athletes and encouraging them when they show that they are working hard also. In addition, as role models, coaches can demonstrate honesty when communicating with their team. It is okay to say that the practice will be difficult but it is something all the team members can achieve.

In other words, not only should practice be planned for skill development, but it should also be age appropriate. The coach is looking to build a confident team that trusts in his or her judgment. If the practice is far beyond the skill level of the team, the athletes will only be left feeling frustrated and insecure in their abilities. So when the coach says, "You can do it," it honestly has to be true.

7

THE PLAYBOOK: BEST PRACTICES—INTERVENTION

Intervention is a very complex issue. It is about dealing with bullying in a manner that protects the victim and demonstrates to the bystanders that bullying behavior is not acceptable in any form. In striving toward good sportsmanship we need to emphasize that bullying behavior will not be tolerated. Bystanders fear they are potentially at risk when bullying behavior occurs so it is essential that we, as adults, prevent the behavior and have clear consequences when the behavior is observed.

Rigby (2007) found that when peers witnessing bullying behaviors object to the bullying, there is a good chance that the behavior will stop. In fact, research indicates that when the bystander simply objects to the behavior it stops about half the time. This supports the notion that effective prevention begins with the bystander. We can change the belief of many students who feel that bullying is part of the way that things are and that everyone has to endure it in some fashion. We can prevent the silence, ignoring of the behaviors, and reluctance to get involved. We can change sayings such as, "It is not my problem" or "He can take care of himself" to "Leave him alone" or "Knock that off."

When it comes to bystanders, there is a small portion that feels it is not okay to bully and is willing to respond to help the victim. The key is to understand why many kids who witness the behaviors do not intervene. By tapping into the bystander's empathy for the victim, we can help bystanders stand up for their peers. We can encourage all bystanders to act at some level that they can be comfortable with, which will help change the social norms related to bullying.

Retaliation for supporting the victim is a real concern for bystanders. This can come in the form of ridicule, humiliation, or actual transfer of the bullying behavior to the bystander. Therefore everyone needs to know that the consequences will be applied to everyone involved and that adults will continue to monitor the situation to prevent future instances. In that way bystanders will know that they are protected for their courage. We know that adults witness less bullying incidents than peers do; therefore we need to help bystanders act to really tackle bullying. The key factors in promoting bystander action are outlined in best practices 5, praise kindness and good sportsmanship, and 6, address bullying consistently and appropriately when it happens.

BEST PRACTICE 5

It is traditional to reward successful behavior in athletics. This happens during the season as well as at the end when achievements, teamwork, and sportsmanship are recognized publically, in front of peers, parents, and coaching staff. When bullying prevention is a part of the program to develop good sportsmanship and strong character, rewards reinforce the behavioral expectations.

When an athlete comes to the rescue of a teammate or peer that has suffered at the hands of a bullying aggressor, the coach should offer praise for the courage and responsible action. This type of kindness, especially receiving positive feedback from coaches, will become contagious. The reinforcement from the coach and other adults as well as teammates will help steer the athletes toward proactive bystander behavior.

BEST PRACTICE 6

Before we can address the problem of bullying, we need to be clear about what it is, so let's again clarify the definition of bullying (Kevorkian, 2006). We know that bullying is an intentional negative action that is power based and is repeated over time. Bullying is behavior that is without justification and often is a source of enjoyment for the perpetrators. Rigby (2007) found that it differs from other conflicts because there is always an imbalance of power between the bully and the victim. This definition applies to every aspect of a student's life including athletics (figure 7.1).

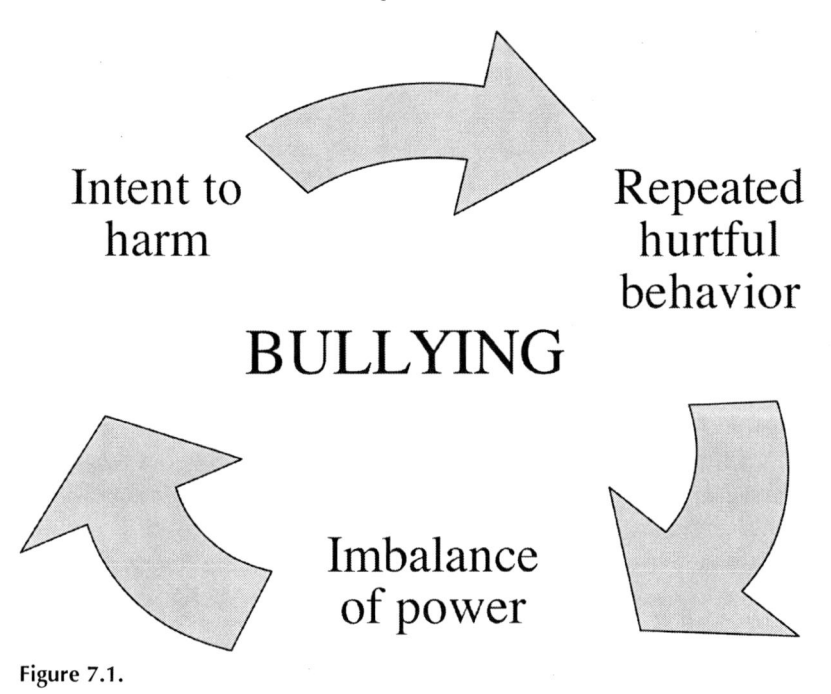

Intent to harm → Repeated hurtful behavior → Imbalance of power

BULLYING

Figure 7.1.

Bullying can be mild or severe; direct (hitting, poking, pushing) or indirect (insults, exclusion, or isolation). Each of these forms of bullying can be expanded upon to many other forms but in any case, bullying occurs when these behaviors exist and there is an imbalance of power.

Bullying can happen anywhere, and that includes the locker room and the playing field. Bullying is when there is exclusion and elitism between team members and team rivals. Bullying is when team members name-call and humiliate each other. Often this is disguised as joking and fun but when there is an imbalance of power because of age, status on the team, or by numbers, it is bullying. In fact in some instances this behavior is considered to be an integral part of team building—a toughening up of the newest members of the team—but it isn't.

Psychologists and male violence experts point out that the same qualities our society accepts that are considered aggressive are the same expectations athletes hold true. We value athletes who are rough, tough, and strong. We want them to pump up for games and destroy their opponents. However these values that are acceptable in the context of the sport are truly not acceptable in any other aspect of society.

For instance, just look at the descriptions of football players taken from the *Boston Globe* online on January 24, 2009: "BC defensive tackle B. J. Raji has been abusing offensive linemen during practice." This is a very common phenomenon. Violent descriptions of athletes, games, and athletic events are commonplace.

If that statement read, "High school student R. J. Someone has been abusing other students during class" it would not be acceptable. This frequent use of violent language makes it difficult to recognize bullying in athletics because of the cultural attitude in athletics that encourages violence.

Competition is extremely important and yet its value is lost in the acceptance of violent language that promotes brutality, meanness, and bullying behavior. Therefore it is important that there be a primary understanding of what constitutes bullying and an agreement that it is not acceptable in the athletic arena despite the common language that implies violence.

Athletic directors, coaches, assistant coaches, and all involved in the athletic program need to have an understanding of bullying and an intention to stop it. Therefore, all participants need to be trained and must have a common understanding of bullying.

When bullying occurs, it needs to be dealt with immediately with a plan for handling these instances. It is best for each athletic department or team league to develop its own plan for handling bullying incidents. How bullying is reported and who is in the best position to oversee the process is best determined by each individual group.

This serves two purposes—it gives people the opportunity to participate in the process and to attend to the uniqueness of each group. Through involvement in the process they will have ownership in the plan. This is essential if there is to be consistency with their response to bullying incidents within the athletic arena.

Most importantly, the staff must listen closely and respond immediately to a student who reports bullying. When a bullying incident occurs the staff needs to look at interventions as an opportunity to teach every member of the team about how bullying can be stopped, rather than treating it strictly as a disciplinary action.

This is totally in sync with the expectations of good sportsmanship yet it brings it to the next level of awareness. Sportsmanship expresses a goal that the sport will be enjoyed for its own sake, with proper consideration and emphasis on fairness, ethics, respect, and a sense of fellowship with one's competitors. Winning is important but it must happen within the context of ethical behavior. The key areas that support sportsmanship and prevent bullying are tied to best practice 7, increase adult supervision; and best practice 8, monitor and continue these efforts in order to sustain the changes over time and to change the climate.

BEST PRACTICE 7

Increase adult supervision in hot spots for bullying. Pay particular attention to athletes who are less skilled as they are more likely to be bullied.

Bullying happens everywhere in school—the classroom, lunchroom, halls, locker room, and bus stop, and the athletic arena is no exception. Bullying can happen anywhere students gather. Now with the Internet the opportunity for bullying, and ultimately the victimization of a student, is even greater.

We know that cyberbullying can happen 24 hours a day, 7 days a week. This level of availability of electronic means to a bully makes it very important that bullying prevention be a part of the athletic setting. Since integrity and character development are integral parts of an athletic program, it makes sense that bullying prevention should be no exception.

Supervision of areas where bullying can occur is essential to reducing this behavior. Attention and visibility on the part of adults are very important. When there is little or no supervision, young people are more likely to victimize teammates. Even though bullying can take place anywhere, there are certain areas where bullying is more likely to occur. These areas are often called *hot spots*.

Identification of these hot spots is the first step in bullying prevention. The easiest way to do this is simply to ask the athletes. After a discussion about bullying, you can ask the students where bullying is most likely to occur. A survey is also a tool that can be used to determine where the bullying is happening.

Before you ask athletes about their experiences regarding bullying, it is important to be certain that they have an understanding of exactly what entails bullying. Therefore the survey needs to begin with a definition of bullying.

> Bullying is an intentional action with the intent to do harm that is repeated over time and involves an imbalance of power.

In other words, bullying is a mean or cruel action that is intended to hurt and injure or humiliate and embarrass someone else. It is bullying when the victim cannot or will not protect himself. It is about a misuse of power. Whatever your choice of words, the definition must be clear. Asking the athletes if they understand will give you the opportunity to clear up any of their confusion about the subject.

It may take some time to help them understand that it is not okay to hurt or humiliate their fellow athletes as part of any ritual—no matter how benign or subtle the activity. However, it is important to get the information in order to increase supervision. Table 7.1 is a sample survey that can be used to determine where bullying may be occurring.

Table 7.1 Informal Bullying Survey for Athletes

	Yes	No	Comments
1. Have you ever seen bullying behavior?			
2. Has it happened between students in your school?			
3. Has it ever happened between team members?			
4. Have you ever been a victim of bullying?			
5. Where did the bullying take place?			
6. Was the bullying physical?			
7. Was the bullying verbal?			
8. Was the bullying cyber (bullying by electronic means)?			
9. Were there any adults that knew about the bullying?			
10. Did anyone try to help?			

This survey can be informal—you can simply ask and record the verbal responses. It can also be given to the athletes in an anonymous setting.

Once the hot spots where bullying has occurred have been identified, steps can be taken to properly supervise these areas. So, for instance, if the bullying is in the locker room, then a coach, assistant, or other adult needs to be present when the athletes are in that area to prevent it. Sustaining this effort is very important. Bullying prevention is not a one-time event—rather, it is an ongoing effort.

BEST PRACTICE 8

Monitor and continue these efforts in order to sustain the changes over time and to change the climate. Checking in and evaluating the effectiveness of the bullying prevention effort is essential. There are several ways to approach this in order to gather the information necessary for its effectiveness. Once again, asking the athletes is a place to begin. The survey can be readministered and the results compared to determine if there is any reduction in bullying. In addition, staff can look at the areas where students are reporting that bullying is occurring and make adjustments in supervision. There may be shifts in the locations where bullying is most likely to occur and identifying them will help you address them as well as the originally identified areas.

Parents and parent support groups are extremely important to gathering data on bullying behaviors. Parents may be not only additional observers of how their athlete is reacting to the discipline and structure of the team but also another source of information on where and when bullying may be occurring. Bullying prevention takes everyone and must be reinforced and evaluated on a continual basis. Training is an ongoing process and staff should be provided continual reinforcement to be updated on bullying prevention techniques. The eight practices discussed here and in chapter 6 should be posted and reviewed regularly until they become an integral part of the athletic program (figure 7.2).

We can tackle bullying in athletics and provide the athletic arena to help kids flourish by stopping it and changing the culture that supports the behavior. In this book we have discussed the dangers associated with bullying behaviors and outlined practices that can prevent bullying. Using these

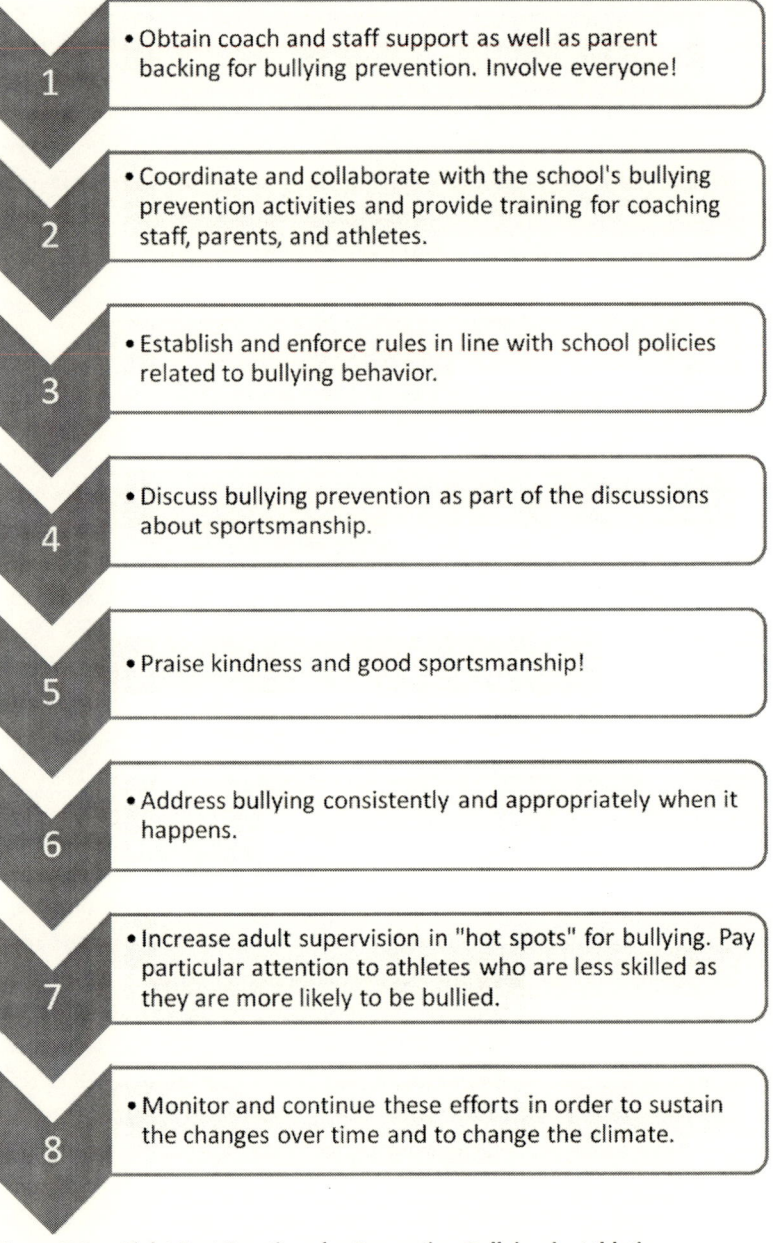

1. Obtain coach and staff support as well as parent backing for bullying prevention. Involve everyone!

2. Coordinate and collaborate with the school's bullying prevention activities and provide training for coaching staff, parents, and athletes.

3. Establish and enforce rules in line with school policies related to bullying behavior.

4. Discuss bullying prevention as part of the discussions about sportsmanship.

5. Praise kindness and good sportsmanship!

6. Address bullying consistently and appropriately when it happens.

7. Increase adult supervision in "hot spots" for bullying. Pay particular attention to athletes who are less skilled as they are more likely to be bullied.

8. Monitor and continue these efforts in order to sustain the changes over time and to change the climate.

Figure 7.2. Eight Best Practices for Preventing Bullying in Athletics

practices, we can start today making certain that we help our children reap the benefits of sports and carry those skills into everyday life and into the future. Athletes can create a positive atmosphere to be shared with fans and all involved in sports.

Athletes often have control on the field and in the game but lose this control in unsupervised and unstructured areas like the locker room, social networks, buses, postgame events, and the virtual world. When this happens, we all have seen and read about the tragic and destructive consequences of bullying. Therefore everyone must not only minimize bullying behavior but also stop it once and for all.

Adults need to be aware and watchful. At the same time, kids need to be clear on what is unacceptable and what is acceptable. This along with clear rules and consequences can and will dramatically decrease bullying behaviors. When everyone has the same understanding of bullying behavior and how to prevent it, the climate changes, and it becomes a win-win situation for all.

When we add the leadership and peer status usually held by athletes, we promote a model for taking a stand against bullying that is carried into the general school population. Most often athletes are looked up to by their peers. The prestige and position of athletes can be used as a powerful positive example of proactive bystanders who stand up and speak up against bullying behavior. This can be the catalyst to change the climate of an entire school.

Families can also have a tremendous impact on athletes to reduce bullying behavior. The only way for you and your family not to become victims is to get involved in bullying prevention. Remember, stepping up to the plate and becoming an active bystander is contagious. Stopping bullying behavior is the winning point.

FINAL THOUGHTS ON PREVENTING BULLYING IN ATHLETICS

Inspirational thoughts on athletics and sportsmanship by role models in the athletic arena are in alignment with the practices and measures suggested in this book. Although the audience for these messages may differ, the messages are similar as they are reflective of the attitude that supports bullying prevention. These reflections may guide you through the perfect season on and off the field.

President Obama, on the loss of the Chicago Olympic bid, October 2, 2009:

> One of the things that I think is valuable about sports is that you can play a great game and still not win.

John Wooden, UCLA basketball coach, with ten national championships:

> Consider the rights of others before your own feelings, and the feelings of others before your own rights.

Don Shula, Football Hall of Fame coach:

> I don't know any other way to lead but by example.

Don R. Kirkendall, PhD, professor emeritus, University of New York; retired evaluator of national sports programs (1978–2005); past president, Research Consortium of the American Alliance of Health, Physical Education, Recreation and Dance (AAHPERD); past president, North American Society of Psychology of Sport and Physical Activity (NASPSPA):

Good sportsmanship is unquestionably the most important aspect of participation in sports by youth. Its importance far surpasses the results of contests, the skill required and/or attained. Without good sportsmanship, participation is rather meaningless in the total scope of things. The sport participant can always gain in physical skill and fitness. However, to make participation and the sport itself meaningful the participant must be taught to practice good sportsmanship.

Just what is good sportsmanship? In many ways, it may be likened to the golden rule; namely "do unto others as you would have others do unto you." This means to treat others with respect and integrity; both your sporting opponents as well as your teammates, officials, coaches and spectators. It means to be courteous and considerate. One should be complimentary to anyone who makes a good play, support and encourage teammates when they may make a mistake. Of course, taunting or ridiculing an opponent is out of order. Remember the golden rule and always ask yourself how you would like to be treated in a similar situation.

A good sport listens intently to coaches and attempts to carry out their instruction. A good sport also respects the decisions made by game officials, even when you are sure the official is wrong.

Being a good sport does not mean that you should not play competitively. An important part of good sportsmanship is to always put forth your very best effort and after the contest is over be a "good loser" or hopefully a gracious winner.

Another statement that perhaps describes the essence of good sportsmanship is the motto of the National Youth Sports Program, which was sponsored by the NCAA and which I had the privilege of working with for more than 25 years. The motto is: WALK TALL, TALK TALL, STAND TALL.

Pauline Finberg, high school cheerleading coach (twenty-nine years); author of *Cheerleading* (Scholastic Press):

As a cheerleading coach for twenty-nine years, I felt the first step I needed to take to have a top performing squad was to teach sportsmanship. What do I mean by sportsmanship? To me it means showing dignity and respect to your coach, fans, and opponents. The squad knew they were a reflection of me, the team, the school, and their parents. When the opponents are yelling obscenities and the tension can be felt by everyone; the spirit of true sportsmanship shows.

Controlling my cheerleaders when everything around us was out of control was not easy. It is at a time like that the foundation of good sportsmanship was so important. After a big tournament hockey game, the opposing fans were so out of control at losing, they spat on me and my squad. At that moment it would have been easy for the cheerleaders to yell, gesture, or spit back. Instead, they all turned their backs on the rude opponents, as the security rushed in to move them away. When we were safely on the team bus, one of the cheerleaders said to me, "I hope you know that it was because of you that I didn't yell something bad at those fans." I thanked the cheerleader but reminded her that she showed respect for herself and the squad, as well as good sportsmanship. Making good sportsmanship second nature to my squad made my job, as their coach, easier. I had to know, if we faced bullying fans, I could depend on my squad to know how to behave. Sportsmanship to me is showing pride in your team, being a leader, and taking responsibility for your actions.

Phil Vaccaro, CMAA, high school athletic director, Athletic Director of the Year 2008:

Good sportsmanship is a value and a conditioned response. It defines who a person is according to how they react to events. When athletes lose their tempers, they are losing their focus. We need to teach them to focus on their best performance rather than what just happened. It is at that point that they make a choice about how they will react. This is when they are able to learn about character, ethics and integrity.

You can change habits even though some people may accept poor sportsmanship behaviors as the norm for sports. This will continue unless the appropriate behaviors we expect as part of good sportsmanship are acknowledged. In our program, we reward good sportsmanship by acknowledging it when we see it. We use printed rewards with our "Sportsmanship is the winning point" logo to promote our message. We have extended that message into the community. In response, some local banks and merchants have responded by subsidizing the cost of some of our training meetings and give-away rewards.

Above all we need to model appropriate behavior. Kids watch more than they listen. We must model the behavior we expect. It makes no sense to talk about values and then yell and scream when we expect the athletes to display good sportsmanship. It is not about fear. It is about respect. We want kids to strive to be the best they can be by looking at us as positive role models. It is about being a teacher first and coach second so that kids will be students first and athletes second. We can teach sportsmanship and that needs to be our primary goal; therefore all coaches must be trained in the fundamentals of good sportsmanship so that they understand the full impact of the influence they have on young athletes.

Our team represents our theme of sportsmanship. Branding is important—it makes the message of good sportsmanship paramount. You will see our message everywhere: on scoreboards; locker room walls; letterhead; even trash cans! It sends a consistent message that is right out there in public for all to see.

Parents know what we stand for and they support our initiative. We teach parents about our message and its importance to youth. They in turn apply peer pressure to other parents at events who may not be behaving appropriately. When everyone is on board and in full agreement, the standard changes and everyone understands and demonstrates the true meaning of good sportsmanship. That is the best thing we can do for our young athletes today!

REFERENCES

Atlas, R., & Pepler, D. (1998). Observations of bullying in the classroom. *Journal of Educational Research*, 92(2), 86.

Beran, T., & Shapiro, B. (2005). Evaluation of an anti-bullying program: Student reports of knowledge and confidence to manage bullying. *Canadian Journal of Education*, 28(4), 700.

Berkowitz, M. W., & Bier, M. C. (2007). What works in character education. *Journal of Research in Character Education*, 5(1), 29.

Brinson, S. (2005). Boys don't tell on sugar-and-spice-but-not-so-nice girl bullies. *Reclaiming Children and Youth*, 14(3), 169.

Burns, S. (2006). School bullying in Northern Ireland: It hasn't gone away you know [Electronic Version]. Young Life and Times Survey. Retrieved January 22, 2008, from www.ark.ac.uk/ylt/2005/.

Chibbaro, J. (2007). School counselors and the cyberbully: Interventions and implications. *Professional School Counseling*, 11(1), 65.

Coloroso, B. (2005). A bully's bystanders are never innocent. *Education Digest*, 70(8), 49.

Craig, W., & Pepler, D. (1997). Naturalistic observations of bullying and victimization on the playground. LaMarsh Centre for Research on Violence and Conflict Resolution, York University.

Craig, W., Pepler, D., & Atlas, R. (2000). Observations of bullying in the playground and in the classroom. *School Psychology International*, 21(1), 22–36.

Craig, W., Pepler, D., & Blais, J. (2007). Responding to bullying: What works? *School Psychology International*, 28(4), 465–77.

Crick, N. R. (1995). Relational aggression: The role of intent attributions, feelings of distress, and provocation type. *Development and Psychopathology*, 7, 313–22.

Crow, B., Ammon Jr., R., & Phillips, D. R. (2004). Anti-hazing strategies for coaches and administrators. *Strategies*, 17(4), 13–15.

References

Dake, J., Price, J., & Telljohann, S. (2003). The nature and extent of bullying at school. *Journal of School Health*, 73(5), 173–80.

Dake, J., Price, J., Telljohann, S., & Funk, J. (2003). Teacher perceptions and practices regarding school bullying prevention. *Journal of School Health*, 73(9), 347.

Dinkes, R., Kemp, J., & Baum, K. (2009). *Indicators of School Crime and Safety: 2008* (NCES 2009–022/NCJ 226343) [Electronic Version]. National Center for Education Statistics, Institute of Education Sciences, U.S. Department of Education, and Bureau of Justice Statistics, Office of Justice Programs, U.S. Department of Justice. Washington, DC. Retrieved from http://nces.ed.gov/pubsearch/pubsinfo.asp?pubid=2009022.

Dufresne, J. (2005). Keeping students and schools safe. *Reclaiming Children and Youth*, 14(2), 93.

Eisenberg, M., Neumark-Sztainer, D., & Perry, C. (2003). Peer harassment, school connectedness, and academic achievement. *Journal of School Health*, 73(8), 311.

Endresen, I. M., & Olweus, D. (2005). Participation in power sports and antisocial involvement in preadolescent and adolescent boys. *Journal of Child Psychology and Psychiatry*, 46(5), 468–78.

Entenman, J., Murnen, T., & Hendricks, C. (2005). Victims, bullies, and bystanders in K-3 literature. *Reading Teacher*, 59(4), 352.

Fekkes, M., Pijpers, F., & Verloove-Vanhorick, P. (2004). Bullying behavior and associations with psychosomatic complaints and depression in victims. *Journal of Pediatrics*, 144, 17–22.

Frisén, A., Jonsson, A.-K., & Persson, C. (2007). Adolescents' perception of bullying: Who is the victim? Who is the bully? What can be done to stop bullying? *Adolescence*, 42(168), 749.

GLSEN. (2001). From teasing to torment: School climate in America [Electronic Version]. Retrieved from www.glsen.org/binary-data/GLSEN_ATTACHMENTS/file/499-1.pdf.

———. (2008). 2007 national school climate survey: Nearly 9 out of 10 LGBT students harassed [Electronic Version]. Retrieved from www.glsen.org/cgi-bin/iowa/all/news/record/2340.html.

Greer, Donald R. (1983). Spectator booing and the home advantage: A study of social influence in the basketball arena. *Social Psychology Quarterly*, 46(3), 252–61.

Halawah, I. (2005). The relationship between effective communication of high school principal and school climate. *Education*, 126(2), 334–45.

Hazler, R., & Miller, D. (2001). Adult recognition of school bullying situations. *Educational Research*, 43(2), 133–46.

Hickey, C. (2003). Bad sports: The risks associated with not "fitting in." *Journal of Physical Education New Zealand*, 36(1), 3.

Hoard, D. (2007). Examining the effects of changing students' attitudes and school ecology on bullying behavior. Unpublished PhD diss., University of Texas at Austin.

Hodges, E., Boivin, M., Vitaro, F., & Bukowski, W. (1999). The power of friendship: Protection against an escalating cycle of peer victimization. *Developmental Psychology*, 35(1), 94–101.

Juvonen, J. (2007). Reforming middle schools: Focus on continuity, social connectedness, and engagement. *Educational Psychologist*, 42(4), 197–208.

Kevorkian, M. (2006). *Preventing bullying: Helping kids form positive relationships.* Lanham, MD: Roman & Littlefield Education.

Klein, J. (2006). Cultural capital and high school bullies: How social inequality impacts school violence. *Men and Masculinities*, 9(1), 53–75.

Kremer-Sadilk, T., & Kim, J. L. (2007). Lessons from sports: Children's socialization to values through family interaction during sports activities. *Discourse and Society*, 18, 35–52.

Kuntsche, E., Pickett, W., Overpeck, M., Craig, W., Boyce, W., & de Matos, M. G. (2006). Television viewing and forms of bullying among adolescents from eight countries. *Journal of Adolescent Health*, 39(6), 908–15.

Lipson, J. (2001). Hostile hallways: Bullying, teasing, and sexual harassment in school. *American Journal of Health Education*, 32, 307–9.

Lodge, J., & Frydenberg, E. (2005). The role of peer bystanders in school bullying: Positive steps toward promoting peaceful schools. *Theory into Practice*, 44(4), 329.

Lumpkin, A. (2008). Teaching values through youth and adolescent sports. *Strategies*, 21(4), 19–23.

Lyznicki, J. M., McCaffree, M. A., & Robinowitz, C. (2004). Childhood bullying: Implications for physicians. *American Family Physician*, 70(9), 1723–28.

Metzler, C., Biglan, A., Rusby, J., & Sprague, J. (2001). Evaluation of a comprehensive behavior management program to improve school-wide positive behavior support. *Education and Treatment of Children*, 24(4), 448.

Mintah, J. K., Huddleston, S., & Doody, S. G. (1999). Justifications of aggressive behavior in contact and semicontact sports. *Journal of Applied Social Psychology*, 29(3), 597–605.

Nansel, T. R., Overpeck, M. D., Pilla, R. S., Ruan, W. J., Simons-Morton, B., & Scheidt, P. (2001). Bullying behaviors among US youth: Prevalence and association with psychosocial adjustment. *Journal of the American Medical Association*, 285, 2094–2100.

Nickelodeon. (2001). Bullying, discrimination and sexual pressures "big problems" for today's tweens and younger kids; parents often wait for their kids to raise tough issues [Electronic Version]. Retrieved January 22, 2008, from www.talkingwithkids.org/nickelodeon/pr-3-8-01.htm.

Nolin, M. J., Davies, E., & Chandler, K. (1995). *Student victimization at school: Statistics in brief.* Washington, DC: National Center for Education Statistics. ED 388 439.

Nucci, C., & Young-Shim, K. (2005). Improving socialization through sport: An analytic review of literature on aggression and sportsmanship. *Physical Educator*, 62(3), 123–29.

Nuwer, H. (2000). *High school hazing: When rites become wrongs.* New York: Franklin Watts.

Ojala, K., & Nesdale, E. (2004). Bullying and social identity: The effects of group norms and distinctiveness threat on attitudes towards bullying. *British Journal of Developmental Psychology*, 22(1), 19–35.

Olweus, D. (1994). *Bullying at school.* New York: Wiley.

Pepler, D. (2006). Bullying interventions: A binocular perspective. *Child and Adolescenct Psychiatry*, 15(1), 16–20.

Piek, J. P., Barrett, N. C., Allen, L. S. R., Jones, S., & Louise, M. (2005). The relationship between bullying and self-worth in children with movement coordination problems. *British Journal of Educational Psychology*, 75, 453–63.

Rhea, D. J., & Lantz, C. D. (2004). Violent, delinquent, and aggressive behaviors of rural high school athletes and non-athletes. *Physical Educator*, 61(4), 170–76.

Rigby, K. (2007). *Bullying in schools and what to do about it* (rev. ed.). Melbourne: ACER Press.

Rigby, K., & Johnson, B. (2006). Bystander's dilemma: Playground heroes. *Greater Good*, 3(2), 10.

Rowe, C. J. (1998). Aggression and violence in sports. *Psychiatric Annals*, 28(5), 265–69.

Salmivalli, C., Kaukiainen, A., & Voeten, M. (2005). Anti-bullying intervention: Implementation and outcome. *British Journal of Educational Psychology*, 75, 465.

Salmon, G., James, A., & Smith, D. M. (1998). Bullying in schools: Self-reported anxiety, depression and self-esteem in secondary school children. *British Medical Journal*, 317, 924–25.

Schinnerer, J. (2009). The consequences of verbally abusive athletic coaches. Psych Central. Retrieved from http://psychcentral.com/lib/2009/the-consequences-of-verbally-abusive-athletic-coaches/.

Schnohr, C., & Niclasen, B. (2006). Bullying among Greenlandic schoolchildren: Development since 1994 and relations to health and health behavior. *International Journal of Circumpolar Health*, 65(4), 305–12.

Shields, D. L., Bredemeier, B. L., LaVoi, N., & Power, F. C. (2005). The sport behavior of youth, parents and coaches: The good, the bad and the ugly. *Journal of Research in Character Education*, 3(1), 43.

Spade, J. A. (2007). The relationship between student bullying behaviors and self-esteem. Unpublished EdD diss., Bowling Green State University, Bowling Green, Ohio.

Storch, E. A., Werner, N. E., & Storch, J. B. (2003). Relational aggression and psychosocial adjustment in intercollegiate athletes. *Journal of Sport Behavior*, 26(2), 155–67.

Sullivan, T. N., Farrell, A. D., & Kliewer, W. (2006). Peer victimization in early adolescence: Association between physical and relational victimization and drug use, aggression, and delinquent behaviors among urban middle school students. *Development and Psychopathology*, 18, 119–37.

Twemlow, S., Fonagy, P., Sacco, F., Gies, M., Evans, R., & Ewbank, R. (2001). Creating a peaceful school learning environment: A controlled study of an elementary school intervention to reduce violence. *American Journal of Psychiatry*, 158(5), 808–10.

Watson, M. (2006). Long-term effects of moral/character education in elementary schools: In pursuit of mechanisms. *Journal of Research in Character Education*, 4(1–2), 1–18.

Williams, T., Connolly, J., Pepler, D., & Craig, W. (2005). Peer victimization, social support, and psychosocial adjustment of sexual minority adolescents. *Journal of Youth and Adolescence*, 34(5), 471.

Wilson, D. (2004). The interface of school climate and school connectedness and relationships with aggression and victimization. *Journal of School Health*, 74(7), 293–99.

Wolley, M., & Bowen, G. (2007). In the context of risk: Supportive adults and the school engagement of middle school students. *Family Relations*, 56(1), 92–104.

ABOUT THE AUTHORS

Meline Kevorkian, Ed.D., is the author or coauthor of several books, including *101 Facts about Bullying: What Everyone Should Know*; *Preventing Bullying: Helping Kids Form Positive Relationships*; *Six Secrets for Parents to Help Their Kids Achieve in School*; and *The Comfort Zone: Providing a Safe and Bully Free Environment for School-Age Child Care*. She is the executive director of academic review at Nova Southeastern University, a former columnist at the Miami Herald, and a board member of the International Bullying Prevention Association. Meline presents regularly on best practices in bullying prevention and cyber bullying, as well as numerous topics facing educators, parents, and students in today's schools. Her experience includes teaching and administrative positions in both public and private schools from preschool through the university level. Her research focuses on best practices in bullying prevention, school safety, and academic achievement. She has been featured on *The Today Show*, CNN, NBC, FOX, CBS, WSVN, *Mom Talk Radio*, WLRN Public Television, BlueSuitMom.com, and the National PTA.

Robin D'Antona, Ed.D., is an educational consultant and adjunct professor at Nova Southeastern University. She is coauthor of *101 Facts about Bullying: What Everyone Should Know* and *The Comfort Zone: Providing a Safe and Bully Free Environment for School Age Child Care*. She is a certified national Olweus bullying prevention trainer and works with school districts, after-school programs, and other groups training parents, teachers, coaches, and practitioners about bullying prevention. Robin frequently presents at conferences on a variety of topics related to school safety. She is a founding board member of the International Bullying Prevention Association, Inc., and is the former associate director of the

Project on Teasing and Bullying at the Center for Research on Women of the Wellesley Centers for Women. In addition, Robin was a program consultant to the Commonwealth of Massachusetts Bullying Prevention Project expansion schools.

PROPERTY OF
BAKER COLLEGE
Owosso Campus

Breinigsville, PA USA
29 September 2010
246291BV00001B/2/P